The Future of the Dollar and the World Reserve System

The Future of the Dollar and the World Reserve System

James Morrell

Butterworths
London Boston Durban Sydney Toronto Wellington

First published 1981

British Library Cataloguing in Publication Data

Morrell, James
The future of the dollar and the world reserve system.
1. Currency question — United States
2. Dollar, American
I. Title
332.4'52 HG538 80-41724

ISBN 0 408 10674 3
ISBN 0 408 10675 1 Pbk

Typeset by Scribe Design, Gillingham, Kent
Printed and bound by Robert Hartnoll Limited
Bodmin, Cornwall

Preface

Developments in the United States are of such great importance to the rest of the world, particularly countries such as the United Kingdom with a heavy dependence on foreign trade, that it is impossible to consider the future of other countries without first having studied the likely course of events in the US.

The professional analyst and forecaster outside the US has of necessity been compelled to become a student of American social forces, political change and economic trends. We are professional US watchdogs and we are critically interested in the future of the US dollar and its implications for the world's reserve system. Hence this particular study.

The forecaster always asserts that the present and the future have their origins in the past. In this instance it has therefore seemed necessary to glance back at the origins and operation of the gold standard, the sterling system and its collapse, the rise of the dollar, the Bretton Woods system and its ultimate break-up in the 1970s. The re-emergence of a system of floating exchange rates in the 1970s in parallel with the growth of a vast international capital market, associated with soaring rates of price inflation, stands in marked contrast to the days of the gold standard based on London. In addition, rapid technical change in communications sets us in an environment where there must be doubts whether history holds any message for us at all in facing up to today's problems.

But the likelihood is that analysts and politicians will look to the past to seek inspiration in finding modern solutions. A hankering after the 'good old days' of relative price stability and stable exchange rates will prompt a close study of what seemed to work then, even if the parallels are inappropriate, for events have marched onwards to produce a totally different order. It is not without significance, for example, that a candidate in the run up to the 1980 US Presidential election has scouted the idea of renewing the link between the dollar and gold. Thus it is appropriate to re-examine the previous gold system for a change along those lines.

The future may unfold in many different ways and the forecaster is unlikely to envisage the complete range of possible outcomes. His best hope is to identify the most likely runners in the futures race and to place his bets accordingly. A central feature of such a set of forecasts has to be an analysis of price inflation, particularly in the US, for success or failure in the struggle to reduce (or even eradicate) inflation will undeniably shape the future of the dollar and the world reserve system.

Writing in 1980, events are moving rapidly. The fight against inflation is on, worldwide. The dollar has made a partial recovery and radical solutions propounded for the reform of the world exchange and reserve system are being viewed in a new light. Important international study groups are at work and important international conferences are scheduled to renew the debates. I have attempted to outline the current debate in the hope that my commentary and forecasts will not be overtaken by decisions reached in the immediate future. Indeed, the current problems seem so profound and the world's political divisions so great that clear-cut early solutions seem to be out of the question. The self-interests of nation states appear to be widely divergent at this time, so much so that the lowest common denominator of compromise is unlikely to be reached quickly; nor is it likely to emerge as a lasting solution.

The literature on the exchange markets, the Eurocurrency capital markets and the problem of monetary and price inflation is voluminous and characterized by lack of agreement on causes and solutions. The author is, therefore, obliged to form his own judgement as to cause and effect. Nevertheless, I gratefully acknowledge my debt to all those writers, in many cases commenting on the problems in the editorial columns of the leading financial journals from day to day. I am particularly grateful to Mr Hilton Clarke for his comments on events in the 1930s drawn from his experience in the Bank of England. For the post-war period the events become very much alive from a recall of one's work as an analyst and forecaster, operating from the vantage point of London, the eye of several of the international storms.

In compiling a short analysis of the various factors bearing on the future of the dollar and the world reserve system, subjects are included which could command separate coverage at book length. I have therefore summarized major subjects, such as the future world economic power structure, and endeavoured to retain the salient features of the subject, keeping in mind the relevance of the material to the forecast. The reader is referred to the bibliography for more detailed study.

Finally, I must record my grateful thanks to my wife Margaret for all her skilled secretarial work in preparing the manuscript as well as coping with an author working against the clock.

James Morrell
May 1980

List of Tables

List of Charts

Contents

1

Gold and the pound sterling

The role of money

From ancient times the use of money has been fostered by governments and the demands of trade. Money is a store of purchasing power as well as the means of exchange and it therefore provides a means of holding reserves, providing purchasing power in an emergency.

Reserves can be held in many forms and a strategic stockpile of materials is just as much a reserve as a holding of gold or foreign currency. We read in Exodus of Pharoah's dream of the seven lean kine devouring the seven fat kine and Joseph's interpretation of that dream leading to the stockpiling of grain in the years of good harvests to meet deficits in the years of bad harvests. In general, however, the increased use of money over the centuries throughout the world, has reduced the need to hold stocks in kind and has almost eliminated barter as a means of exchange. Money offers advantages over barter and payments in kind in that it offers a choice of items to be purchased as well as the option to defer purchases through the build-up of a cash reserve.

Not only have traders favoured the use of money because of the flexibility afforded by money payments compared with a straight exchange of goods, but governments, needing to levy taxes to provide supplies to maintain an administrative labour force and to raise armed forces, have found it easier to use money in payment of taxes rather than goods. An interesting example of taxes levied in kind is to be found in the financing during the Hundred Years' War by Edward III of the cost of the army and subsidies to his allies. In 1339 Parliament granted the King a subsidy of the tenth lamb, fleece and sheaf[1]. The King was therefore obliged to enter directly into international trade to raise funds via the sale of the produce since he needed payment in money acceptable both at home and abroad.

In this instance the internationally accepted currency was the gold florin of Florence. The Florentine bankers dominated European commerce at that time and had already introduced the letter (or bill) of exchange. Prior to that the Byzantine besant formed an international currency throughout Europe, though few were minted after the early thirteenth century and by the middle of the century they had become scarce.

[1]FEAVEARYEAR, A. E. (1931). *The Pound Sterling*, p. 14. Oxford University Press.

The pound sterling goes back earlier still and was introduced in Anglo-Saxon times[2]. Originally, the English penny gained general acceptance throughout the Saxon kingdoms, 240 of them being known as a pound. Although the weight varied, the intention was that a pound of money should be equal to a pound weight of silver. When silver was weighed it was reckoned in pounds, shillings and pence. William the Conquerer established his principal mint at the Tower of London and adopted a pound weight, which had been in use before the Conquest, naming this the Tower pound. Early in the twelth century the silver penny was called a sterling. Because of their consistent fineness the coins gained a sound reputation on the Continent and sterling silver ultimately became the silver of commerce in a large part of the world.

The penny was a practical unit for every day transactions and was cut into halves, quarters and even less for use in small transactions. The pound itself, however, was subdivided differently for accounting purposes and ultimately the shilling of 12 pence was adopted, giving a pound divided into 20 shillings and 240 pence. This unit of account continued until replaced by the decimal system in 1971, thus breaking a continuous unit of account going back nearly a thousand years.

The pound sterling has been in continuous use longer than any other currency. Based on silver, some idea of price inflation can be gained by comparing the present price of silver with the original pound. The price of silver has risen 250-fold, indicating an annual average rate of inflation of 0.55% per annum — far less than may generally be supposed.

It is important to distinguish between money as a unit of account and money acceptable in international transactions. Day to day commerce in towns and villages required an accepted unit of account and a convenient form of specie. For such a purpose the pound, with its division into shillings and pence, proved ideal and silver was a realistic choice for the coinage. By contrast, gold has never been a practical basis for a common coinage since its value has been too high for daily and weekly domestic transactions. For example, a gold coin has roughly corresponded in value to a farm worker's weekly wages down the centuries, the same being more or less true to this day in Britain. It will be obvious that such a valuable coin would not be generally acceptable, first because of risk of loss and secondly because of the immediate need to get rid of the gold coin and to break it down into usable 'small' change. Hence attempts to introduce gold coins as common currency for domestic trade have never been generally successful and governments have resoted to silver and other metals for common currency.

For large deals, however, gold was far superior to silver. Thus international payments tended throughout the Middle Ages to be made in gold. Ultimately gold bullion in large value denominations proved still more convenient, although in more recent times paper money and government securities have both supplemented the domestic currency and taken over the role of gold in international settlements.

A particular feature of the history of coinage and currencies is the power of public acceptability. Rulers and governments have frequently attempted changes and reforms but have frequently failed. Old habits die hard and established custom is difficult to break. Notably governments have failed, in spite of draconian and barbarous penalties, from preventing the clipping of

[2]FEAVEARYEAR, A. E. *The Pound Sterling*, p.7.

coins. Currencies were perpetually debased, coins of half weight in some instances passing as currency. Not until the introduction of the milled coin was the abuse halted.

From time to time old currency was called in to be replaced by a recoinage. The tendency was for a lower weight per unit of money to be adopted, thus devaluing the currency while maintaining the accepted units of account. However, it was necessary to have regard to the international price of gold and silver. Where domestic values of gold and silver in the coinage moved out of line with values abroad, then the coins would move in or out of the country or be melted down if the value of the metal exceeded the value of the coin. Again, for many centuries fierce penalties were imposed on the export of coin and on clipping, melting and counterfeiting, all to no avail. In other words, market forces remained paramount.

This characteristic of human behaviour, indicating the power of market forces, is reflected in modern times. We see governments attempting to regulate exchange rates, or the price of gold, or the internal money supply, or prices, or import duties and yet we see their actions sometimes overturned by international market forces. Confidence has been critical at all times and in most instances confidence, or lack of it, has been soundly based on fundamental values and powerful market forces. Thus in modern times the rise of the dollar and decline in the pound have reflected the realities of commercial life. Confidence in the Swiss franc or the deutschemark have rested on confidence in the likelihood of price inflation remaining low by international standards in Switzerland and Germany. This feature, namely the power of market forces and the rule of confidence, is vital in considering the future of the world monetary and reserve system, which is the main concern of this study.

The expansion of trade

It is essential, however, to see how the present state of international commerce, currency and exchange has evolved over time, the factors which have contributed to those changes and the forces now at work which will shape future developments.

Technical change, particularly the speeding-up of transport and communications, plus the expansion of population and commerce, have had the most powerful influence on the pattern and nature of transactions. Throughout the Middle Ages change was slow — indeed, imperceptible by modern standards. Death rates tended to match birth rates — epidemics, plague, starvation brought on by crop failure, diseases and extreme levels of infant mortality combining to hold populations in check at low levels. Again, by today's standards most parts of the world were severely under-populated. With a relative abundance of land, therefore, medieval communities were for the most part self-sufficient. The need to obtain goods from outside the village was rare and trade and commerce accounted for only a small part of the community's product.

Even the church communities tended to be self-sufficient, so that demand for more sophisticated products was restricted to that narrow section of society comprising the feudal aristocracy and the ruler's court. The growth of a commercial class, and of towns and cities with their specialist trades, expanded the market for traded goods. War, too, with the need for arms and supplies probably contributed to the growth of commerce. Even so, both internal and external trade can only have expanded at a minute rate having regard to the virtually static population levels and the general lack of technical progress. Improvements in labour productivity, for example, were rare and productivity can scarcely have changed from generation to generation.

Nevertheless, at those low levels of commerce, the principles of money accounting and exchange between countries became firmly established, based on gold for external transactions and silver for commonplace internal transactions. The letter of exchange obviated the need for costly transportation of specie to cover all transactions and the shorter transit time for letters, being speedier than the transport of gold coin—with all its attendant risks—contributed to the mechanics of foreign and internal trade.

A basis had thus been created for the expansion of commerce and trade. With an embryonic system spreading from Florence to Flanders, other Italian cities, Paris and London, a more sophisticated exchange system was becoming feasible. But expansion, of course, brought with it a rising demand for bullion and from time to time in the Middle Ages a shortage of bullion, tending to push up the value of money and reduce prices, was responsible for contractions of trade. Thus the Spanish discoveries of gold and silver in the Americas began to provide Europe with an increase in the potential money supply in the sixteenth century which coincided with the discovery of sea routes to distant parts of the world. The grounds were then laid for the expansion of trade and commerce. The Spanish and Portuguese colonized South and Central America and parts of Africa and the Spanish established a route across the Pacific to the Phillipines.

At the same time, the Dutch East India trade was founded and the British and French began to colonize North America. With the flood of Spanish gold and silver continuing to pour into Europe in the seventeenth century, the expansion of mercantile trade continued. Trading posts were established in India and there was intense rivalry for the much prized East India trade.

It is also significant that mediaeval Europe, comprising a collection of principalities and city states under the hegemony of the Roman Catholic Church, was being superseded by a system ultimately comprising nation states. The pace of change began to accelerate and with the development of printing and spread of learning the foundations were being laid for the technical and industrial growth of later centuries. That being said, it must not be assumed that the expansion of trade and commerce from the sixteenth century resulted in a significant improvement of living standards. The gradual rise in total output was matched by growth in population, and the benefits in terms of a broadening range of products available to the rich spread down extremely slowly to the poorer parts of society. For what such statistics are worth, the standard of living of the labourer remained much the same throughout the Middle Ages to the nineteenth century and it was only from about 1870 in Europe that a broadly based improvement in average living standards began.

In the interval the development of centralized nation states gave rise to an increasing demand for funds on the part of governments. War was growing more costly and increases in taxation tended to speed up the general use of money. Increased government borrowing must have contributed to the growth of banking systems and the acceptance of paper money as a means of exchange. The changes were most vivid in England in the reign of Henry VIII, where the dissolution of the monasteries and despoliation of the church were means of replenishing the King's coffers. In addition there were major debasements of the currency through recoinages, the King pocketing large profits through his monopoly of issuing new coins. The age of deficit financing had begun, with its attendant price inflation.

Gold and silver

Since gold and silver were eminently suitable for use as coin, both metals have been acceptable as money, silver featuring principally as a domestic means of exchange and gold as a means of settlement for capital transactions and international trade. But because of the acceptability of both metals in most parts of the world as a store of value, a bi-metal standard was in operation throughout the Middle Ages, the relative prices of gold and silver fluctuating with the supply of the metals. Where the value attached to a coin by the authorities fell below what the metal content would fetch at market prices determined by international supply and demand, coin would be melted down or exported, with consequences for the domestic money supply. Generally, any shortfall of coin was made good by the activities of the counterfeiters. Thus governments have always been confronted with complex problems in money management.

Since discoveries of gold and silver have always been haphazard, it has therefore been impossible to plan a permanently stable money system based on those metals. The extensive import of silver via Spain into Europe in the seventeenth century in particular depressed the price of silver in terms of gold. Another complicating factor was the considerable appetite for silver in India. As the Dutch and British East India trade expanded in the seventeenth and eighteenth centuries, demand for silver in the East led European traders to export silver in payment for the luxury goods imported back to Europe. Even so, silver was at a substantially higher price in terms of gold in India than in Europe and within Europe itself the gold/silver ratio was seldom uniform[3].

Against such a complex background it was hardly surprising that a single standard became desirable and that gold ultimately filled that role. In Britain the golden guinea was introduced in 1663 at £3.14s.2d. to the ounce[4]. The weight of the coin of 129.4 gr. was never altered and the small gold coin with the little elephant formed an important new standard. To link up the value of money as closely as possible with the value of metal, it was essential to 'cleanse' the existing currency with a recoinage and to establish that bullion presented to the mint would be converted into coin without charge. Machinery was necessary for regularly withdrawing from circulation old and worn coins for reminting—a reminder of the permanent problem of operating a currency gold standard. In addition, restrictions on the export of English coin needed to be lifted. In this way the internal currency could remain fixed in terms of gold and international demand for the English guinea would in effect directly influence the British money supply. In broad terms, an adverse balance of payments

[3]At the end of the seventeenth century the mint ratio of silver to gold was about 16 to one in Spain against nine to ten to one in the East; FEAVEARYEAR, A. E. *The Pound Sterling*, p.139.
[4]Ibid, p.90.

would contract the money supply and deflate internal spending power. This, in turn, would tend to eliminate the balance of payments deficit.

These, then, were the beginnings of the gold standard system which, with many tribulations, gained in influence up to 1914.

The evolution of the British gold standard

The coinage remained in a chaotic condition in Britain after the introduction of the new guinea in 1663, due to the continued practice of clipping. Moreover, the beginnings of credit banking and the needs of war financing towards the end of the century complicated money management still further. Thus it was not until the general introduction of the milling process and a further massive recoinage operation that something like a workable gold standard became feasible.

In the interim, the guinea valued internally at 20s. in 1663 had risen at one point to 30s[5]. It was called down to 22s. again in the recoinage of 1696 but the valuation of silver in relation to gold in England perpetuated a tendency to export silver coin and to import gold. The consequent shrinkage of silver coin in circulation inhibited trade and following Sir Isaac Newton's famous report on the problem[6], the price of the guinea was reduced in 1717 to 21s. Heavy imports of gold still persisted, resulting in substantial new issues of gold coins and the complete disappearance of full weight silver coins. The gradual acceptance of this situation led to a position by the middle of the eighteenth century where gold had definitely displaced silver so that the British gold standard can be said to date from the fixing of the price of the guinea at 21s. in 1717.

The gold standard was not consciously nor deliberately established. It evolved in the day to day process of attempting to manage a chaotic monetary system to meet the needs of the time. The guinea was used not only for international settlements, but internally in all avenues of trade and commerce. In the newly emerging banking industry, guineas formed an important part of the reserves of the bankers. The tax collectors preferred guineas to bad silver, so that apart from day to day transactions requiring small change, the gold coin became the accepted unit of commerce.

In the meantime credit banking had made important strides. From the formation of the Bank of England in 1694 and the growth of public debt, bank notes became an increasing part of the currency. Watermarked notes reduced the risk of forgery. Private bankers' notes and Bank of England bills and notes began to be supplemented by drafts or cheques. The inland bill of exchange was introduced to facilitate provincial manufacture and trade so that throughout the eighteenth century paper money and credit expanded along with gold as the monetary base of the community.

Bank notes and credit, however, remained attached to gold insofar as banks held a reserve backing of gold. This meant that bank credit was expanded or contracted as the gold reserve itself changed. The growth of banking and bank credit thus led in the nineteenth century to marked swings in the trade cycle,

[5]FEAVEARYEAR, A. E. *The Pound Sterling*, p.120.
[6]NEWTON, Isaac (1717). *Mint Reports*. Sir Isaac Newton was appointed Master of the Mint in 1699.

periodic contractions resulting in panics, crashes, bank failures and the collapse of business houses. In other words, balance of payments movements leading to an outflow of gold led to a contraction of bank credit and what we now call a credit squeeze.

One of the most spectacular contractions occurred at the end of the Napoleonic Wars when the disbandment of the armed forces and the consequent cut in government spending contributed to a severe deflation. In the meantime the inflation and loss of gold during the wars had caused considerable public concern and the whole question of the currency was examined by the Bullion Committee in 1810.

The Bank of England had ceased payments in gold in 1797 and bank notes became legal tender in lieu of gold. Small denomination notes were issued and the wartime crisis (the country was then threatened with invasion) enabled the authorities to introduce the expedient shift to a paper currency with the minimum of dislocation. However, the cost of the war and the balance of payments deficit pushed up the price of gold and drove the exchange rate against the pound.

The Bullion Report, issued in June 1810, concluded that the unfavourable movement of the exchange rate and the rise in the gold price had been caused by an over-issue of Bank of England notes. It was recommended that the convertibility of notes should be restored.

In fact the proposals were rejected by the House of Commons. Bank notes had become increasingly popular and an attempt in 1817 to resume cash payments in gold and to replace smaller denomination notes of £1 and £2 failed, the public preferring notes to gold. At the same time, a further recoinage had become necessary and in July 1817 the world famous sovereign of 20s. was issued for the first time, exactly one hundred years from the introduction of the guinea at 21s.

Then in 1819 a parliamentary committee, under Peel's chairmanship, was formed to re-examine the currency question, its recommendations being embodied in an Act of Parliament[7], providing for the resumption of Bank of England payments in gold, notes being exchangeable for gold on demand at the rate of £4.1s. per ounce of standard gold, ultimately to be £3.17.10½d. per ounce from May 1823. The Act also provided for the removal of penalties on melting and exporting coin and it became legal for any person to export gold and silver coins, to melt them and to sell the resultant bullion. The consequence of the new system was that the Bank of England, a private company, was left with the virtual responsibility of maintaining the national currency. Although the Bank's directors argued that the affairs of the nation were the concern of Parliament, their protests were ignored. Full convertibility at the old standard was achieved within two years; so the gold standard was resumed and in a most rigorous form.

There is one aspect of events in this period which should be of particular interest with regard to the contemporary debate regarding the money system. The attempt to restore the old standard and exchange rate entailed the contraction of credit and forced a reduction in prices. Falling prices enhance the value of debt capital, so that the owners of property benefit in terms of increasing real value of fixed rents and interest receipts. Tenants, on the other

[7]59 George III C 49, dated 2 July 1819, generally known as Peel's Act.

hand, are worse off and a large part of the business community, operating on credit, is also adversely affected. There is therefore a natural tendency or bias for deflation to be resisted by the majority of the community and for expansion and rising prices to be more generally acceptable. A parallel example is to be observed in the deflation following the First World War.

The classical gold standard

The Act of 1820 established the pound on a basis which was virtually an automatic metallic standard, something not achieved either before or since. Various changes over the previous 150 years had made this possible, technical developments regarding the coinage being particularly important. The introduction of the milled edge, the fact that gold was more difficult to counterfeit than silver, and the improvement in crime detection—all contributed to stabilizing the coinage. Moreover, paper money had become generally accepted, thus reducing the dependence on coin for commercial transactions. The centuries old concern for building up and holding a treasure of gold and silver had faded away and there was now little concern whether gold moved in or out of the country. At the lower levels of daily commerce, token coinage had been introduced and accepted, the intrinsic metallic value of the coins being less than their face value.

The system operated with the Bank of England acting as agent for the Mint in purchasing gold bullion and issuing the coins. The Bank was prepared to buy all bullion presented to it. If the value of gold fell elsewhere in the world, large amounts flowed into London. Conversely, internal price inflation, depreciating the value of money, led to an outflow of bullion and gold coins.

Comparatively small movements in the relative price of gold, or in internal costs and prices, led to sharp and substantial movements of gold in or out of the country. It will be seen, therefore, that a powerful regulatory force had been established, the more so since a pyramid of paper money and bank credit rested on a narrow gold base. There were hundreds of small banks up and down the country, completely unregulated and free to back their own judgements in the expansion of their note issues and credits. Credit was uncontrolled so that a credit and money expansion, contributing to a boom, would tend to generate domestic price inflation as well as a payments deficit, the two features driving out gold. The fall in gold holdings contracted the credit base and the cyclical bubble was burst.

The extremities of the cycle under the gold standard in this form clearly called for further reform so far as credit management was concerned. After the great depression following the Napoleonic Wars there was a boom in 1824–1825, followed by a crash and a run on the banks. Cobbet commented :

> The Bank is blamed for putting out paper and causing high prices; and blamed at the same time for not putting out paper to accommodate merchants and keep them from breaking. It cannot be blamed for both, and indeed it is blamable for neither. It is the fellows that put out the paper and then break that do the mischief[8].

[8]COBBETT, William, (1830). *Rural Rides in the Counties of Surrey, Kent, Sussex, etc.*, Vol ii, p.25.

The argument has a contemporary ring about it.

From the crisis the concept emerged of a central bank acting as lender of last resort, using Bank Rate as a regulator. Even so, extreme swings in the trade cycle persisted. The railway boom of the 1830s was followed by a collapse. There was then a period of broad based industrial prosperity in the early 1840s, leading to a second wave of railway mania. The inevitable crash was not long in coming, worsened in its effects by the disastrous harvests and the potato famines of 1845 and 1846[9].

It will be seen, therefore, that the gold standard system was far from adequate as an automatic regulator without the backing of a sophisticated form of credit regulation. Such a system evolved, partly through trial and error and then through commercial legislation. Yet to see the problems of those years in perspective it is important to recognize that Britain's trade and commerce were expanding at what was then an unprecedented pace. By 1850 roughly half the world's trade in manufactures was in British hands. In the 1840s Britain produced 68% of the world's output of coal, 50% of its pig iron, 70% of its steel and 50% of its cotton goods. Britain was by far the world's largest copper producer and in mining as a whole her volume of output increased nearly sixfold in the first half of the nineteenth century, with nearly 300 000 people employed in these industries in 1851.

The origins of this expansion can be traced in the previous century. The Napoleonic Wars had left Britain mistress of the seas. Having lost an empire in North America, she was developing a vast empire in other parts of the world. From the base of a successful agricultural revolution, the industrial revolution, based on iron and steam power, was accompanied by a rapid expansion of primary industries. Britain was a developing country, with a burgeoning population rising from 13 million in 1801 to 27 million by 1851.

Whereas some 36% of the working population worked on the land in 1801, the proportion had dropped to 22% by 1851. Abundant cheap industrial labour and rapid urban development fed the expansion. Thus, with investment and exports forming a large part of the national product, it was perhaps inevitable that swings in the trade cycle would be relatively large and certainly greater than in the developed economy of the late twentieth century.

But the heyday of the gold standard system was yet to come. The expansion of British trade, accompanied by the growth of British shipping, overseas banking, insurance, the building of foreign railways and investment overseas, led in the second half of the nineteenth century to London becoming by far the pre-eminent commercial centre and capital market of the world. The stability of the currency, attributable to the gold standard system, fostered the growth of business in sterling. The bill on London was used for financing not only British trade with the rest of the world, but third country trade also. Thus, in spite of the industrial expansion of the United States, Germany, France and other countries later in the century, London remained the hub of the international markets up to 1914. The Bank of England stood at the centre of the international financial world; sterling and the British gold standard provided the instruments for a stable and successful world exchange and reserve system.

[9]The extremities of the business cycle in the first half of the nineteenth century are brilliantly illustrated in the novels of Dickens, Disraeli, Mrs Gaskell, *et al.*

That system withstood the shocks of periodic crises. The crash in the US in 1857, following the first phase of railway development, had severe repercussions in the United Kingdom, where investors held more than half the stock of the American railway capital. There was widespread failure of US banks and there were severe repercussions in the UK. The links and interdependence of the UK and US economies were steadily growing. This was further illustrated with the effects of the cotton famine during the Civil War in North America.

The reconstruction boom following the Civil War gave way to the prolonged and deep recession of the 1870s in the UK and it is interesting to speculate whether the dominant role given to gold had any bearing on that development. The Californian gold discoveries of 1849 added to the world's gold supply and thereby contributed to a monetary expansion which would have fostered the growth of industry and trade. Without a regular supply of new gold, monetary expansion would have been restricted, since the note issue and bank credit were related to the size of the gold base. The next major expansion of gold supply came with the South African discoveries. Bullion began to reach the market in large quantities in 1893 and in the following year the Bank of England's gold stocks rose to a record £39 million, with another £31 million in the banking reserve. There was then an abundance of money market funds for several years, driving interest rates to an all-time low until the outbreak of the South African War in 1899.

At the same time, the expansion of trade throughout the world posed problems for the UK in that the widespread use of sterling led to foreigners keeping balances in London. Problems abroad, therefore, resulted in periodic heavy calls on the London gold reserves, for it must be remembered that the gold standard also operated in other industrial countries. The difficulties in managing the system were considerable and calls for gold from one centre to another could provoke a credit crisis for no obvious domestic reason. To meet a shortage of gold in London, for example, London banks would call on the gold reserves of their subsidiaries in Australia. Earlier in the century, when the sailing time between Britain and Australia could be as long as several months, a crisis in London could affect Australia virtually 'out of the blue' as a ship arrived months later bearing instructions for gold to be shipped to London[10].

There were, therefore, problems associated with the role of reserve currency and it has to be considered whether the commercial advantages in terms of an international banking industry and a world capital market, with the income so generated by the City of London, balanced the effects on domestic trade imposed by cyclical fluctuations in other countries. The same problem can be observed today and countries such as Switzerland, Germany and France—and more recently the UK—have all sought to avoid the role of a reserve currency. This is a problem to be examined in connection with the future of the world's reserve system.

The swings in the trade cycle, through which the gold standard functioned in its uneasy way, are illustrated in *Chart 1.1* below. This was produced in 1872 to show the peaks and troughs of the cycle in Britain since the Napoleonic Wars. The terminology is revealing, showing panics or crashes with alternate cycles

[10]For an interesting account of the vicissitudes of banking in Australia in the nineteenth century, *see* BLAINEY, G. (1958). *Gold and Paper*, Melbourne—marking the centenary of the foundation of the National Bank of Australasia.

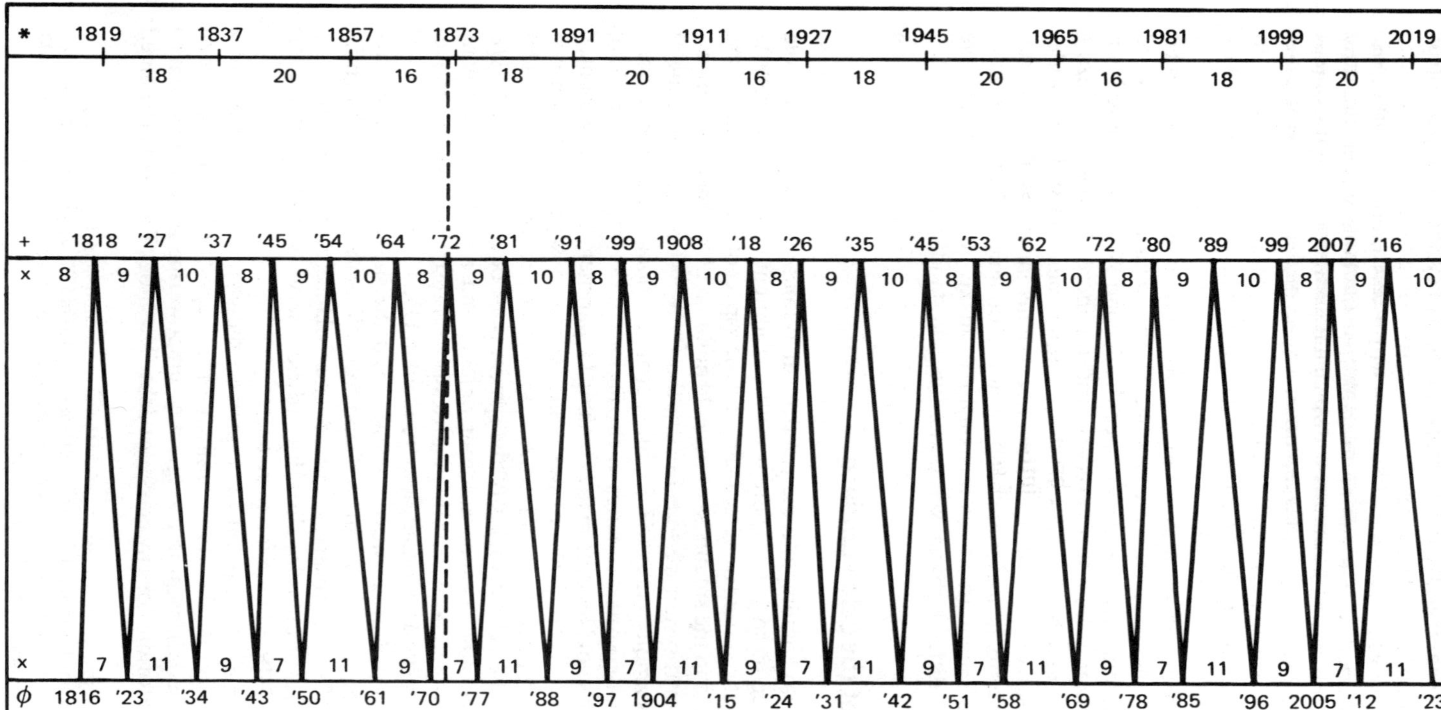

* Years in which panics have occurred and will occur again. Their regular cycles are 16, 18 and 20 years.

+ Years of GOOD TIMES, high prices, and the time to sell stocks and values of all kinds. Their cycles are 8, 9 and 10 years.

ϕ Years of HARD TIMES, low prices, and a good time to buy stocks, corner lots, goods etc., and hold until the chart reached the years of good times, and then unload. Their cycles are 9, 7 and 11 years.

x Intervals in years.

Chart 1.1 Good and bad times — compiled in 1872

(roughly every 20 years) and with the average length of cycle from top to top or bottom to bottom of about ten years, thus corresponding to the sunspot cycles which affect the world's weather. Since the world was predominantly agricultural in that period, it is tempting to think that the cycle was dictated by fluctuations in harvests and food prices. From what we have seen of the swings in credit associated with the gold standard, the agricultural argument has less force and, in any case, with the opening up of American grain supplies to Europe later in the century, bad harvests in Europe could then be mitigated by those supplies.

The author of the chart projected the cycles for another hundred years and it will be seen that his forecasts were falsified by the impact of the two world wars[11]. More significantly, the cycles since the Second World War have been far shorter, averaging four to five years, and far more shallow. Stabilizing factors brought about by the pursuit of full employment policies, the widespread introduction of generous social security systems and the vastly increased roles of governments in national spending and economic management have transformed the scene. In effect this ought to make international reserve management less difficult than it was under the gold standard.

The collapse of the gold standard

It is astonishing to contemplate the relative smoothness with which the gold standard operated up to 1914. There was little argument up to that point as to the suitability of the system or of replacing it. One aspect of the efficiency of the system is reflected in the smallness of the gold holdings of the Bank of England on which the world system rested. In 1913 the Bank of England's holding of coin and bullion amounted to £37.5 million against a domestic money supply, comprising bank deposits and notes in circulation, of £991 million—a ratio of 3.8%. The Bank's gold holding in the Banking Department Reserve amounted to £26.5 million, a mere 2.8% of the domestic money supply[12]. When it is considered that an international reserve system rested on such a slender reserve of gold, the achievements of the system must be acknowledged to be more than remarkable. France had four times as much gold, and Germany twice as much as the UK; yet both countries placed restrictions on the movement of gold compared with complete freedom in UK.

The First World War, however, transformed the international monetary system beyond recognition. As in the Napoleonic Wars there was a substantial drain on the UK's gold reserves. An adverse balance of payments and the raising of subsidies or loans for allies drained the reserves in both instances, the problems in 1914–1918 being far more acute.

The general fear of a run on the banks on the outbreak of war led to a three-day extension of the Bank Holiday of 3 August 1914 and an Act of Parliament, rushed through in a single day, empowering the Government to proclaim a moratorium for any classes of debt. The Stock Exchange remained

[11]I am indebted to Henry Cooke Lumsden, the Manchester stockbrokers, for permission to reproduce this chart which hangs in their office. It was compiled in 1872 by a partner who is believed to have been involved in raising capital for the steel company, John Summers. He would thus have been acutely aware of the trade cycle.

[12]FEAVEARYEAR, A. E. *The Pound Sterling*, p.297.

closed and similar measures were adopted by other countries. The fears of a sudden flight from paper money and a demand for gold led to another hasty Act and on 6 August the Treasury was empowered to issue £1 and 10s. currency notes to be legal tender as fully as sovereigns and half-sovereigns for any amount and convertible at the Bank of England into gold coin on demand.

In the event, the general public did not panic. Notes gradually took the place of gold coin in circulation and the Bank of England expanded its gold holdings. A first important step had been taken in weakening the gold standard system.

The demands of the war led to large purchases of arms and supplies from the US as well as the loss of important export markets. During 1915 and 1916 £49 million of gold was exported, after a gain of £28 million in 1914. The exchange rate against the US dollar began to decline and as gold coins ceased to circulate, a premium on gold began to develop. Towards the end of 1916 a regulation was issued forbidding the melting down or breaking up any gold coin then in use as a currency in any country. In 1917 the export of gold was effectively stopped, virtually all vessels using British ports being under direct government control so that the authorities were able to refuse cargo space for gold.

In addition, an arrangement was reached with South Africa whereby gold producers were compelled to sell all their output to the Bank of England at a price of 77s.9d. As a result there ceased to be a free market in gold in Britain, the Government controlling gold stocks in the interests of war financing and the balance of payments. The US, however, succeeded in maintaining an effective gold standard, even though price inflation (less than in the other belligerent countries) led to an appreciation of the dollar. For its part, the UK Government supported the pound in order to hold down the cost of imports from the US. It also 'borrowed' privately-owned US and Canadian securities to sell, or use as collateral, to raise dollars for war purposes—a manoeuvre that was repeated in the Second World War.

By a variety of means the exchange rate was thus held at an artificially high rate around $4.77. The French franc was also pegged to the pound, the Dutch florin was controlled and the Italian lira and Russian rouble were assisted to prevent large falls.

From all this it would appear that the gold standard had been abandoned and without legislation. The day of the gold sovereign of 20s. had lasted exactly 100 years, just as its predecessor the guinea. Notes had gained universal acceptance and from this feature alone it was exceedingly unlikely that the gold standard could ever be resurrected in its old form. Apparently the public did not want gold coins as currency.

Wartime inflation and the inflationary boom immediately following the ending of hostilities created wide disparities between the major countries. With Germany subjected to heavy reparations payments, Austria dismembered, Russia removed from international commerce by revolution, France and the UK saddled with a huge volume of war debt, there could be no question of returning to pre-war exchange parities. The US economy, by contrast, had strengthened enormously in relation to other countries. As a neutral her balance of payments had strengthened because of the heavy demands for her commodities and manufactured goods. Her industries were better placed to expand into world markets after the war. Her growing population provided advantages in terms of mass production and economies of scale to a greater extent than in the European countries. The dominance of the UK, London and sterling was therefore at an end; in terms of international trade and capital transactions the US had taken the lead.

The inter-war period

From the UK's point of view there was some similarity in the immediate post-war period with the years following the ending of the Napoleonic War in 1815. There had been in both instances a substantial paper money inflation. The gold standard had been suspended or abandoned and there was widespread interest in financial and political circles for a return to old values as represented by the gold standard system. In both cases there had been substantial deflation, unemployment and distress as wartime government spending was slashed and armies disbanded (preceded by rapid inflation immediately after the First World War). In 1920 the Government took a calculated risk in fixing the price of gold low enough to cause a further deflationary squeeze. In 1925 the Government made a similar move, restoring the pound's exchange rate against the dollar at the high rate of $4.867 (the 1914 parity) as a consequence of returning to a gold standard of £3.17s.10½d. per ounce.

The Cunliffe Committee[13], recommending the return to the gold standard, completely ignored the evidence of the 1820s. It began its deliberations before the war had ended and it outlined conditions and some sort of plan for returning to gold at the old standard, regardless of the implied deflation. It recommended the establishment of a sinking fund to reduce the huge quantity of government debt. Legal limits on the note issue were to be re-introduced, but the circulation of gold was to be prevented. All gold in the country was to be concentrated in the Bank of England's reserve and it was recommended that the reserve be built up to £150 million as a pre-condition to returning to gold.

The other European wartime powers, however, made no attempt to raise the values of their currencies. The German currency collapsed under a runaway inflation (not unconnected with the reparations demands imposed by the Allies). Exchange rates fluctuated wildly, the pound having fallen to a low point of $3.19 in 1920. It was against that background that plans were laid for a return to the old standard. The pressures for such a move were not entirely domestic. South Africa was anxious to see a return to gold and Switzerland, the Netherlands and other countries awaited a lead from the UK. It was thus, after a build-up of the gold reserve, that Winston Churchill as Chancellor of the Exchequer, announced in his Budget speech in 1925 that the UK was to return to gold.

The experiment was shortlived. Overtaken by the world crisis and the slump following the Wall Street crash, the UK's balance of payments reached a parlous state. The pound had been over-valued and exports had slumped in a number of key industries. The crisis of 1931 brought down the minority Labour Government; its successor promptly went off gold and devalued the pound. The gold standard was dead. In the continuing depression the US also devalued, raising the price of gold in 1934 from $22.67 to $35 an ounce, a price maintained for over 30 years.

[13] *The Cunliffe Committee Fiscal Report* (Cmnd 464) (December 1919), Her Majesty's Stationery Office, London. Lord Cunliffe was Governor of the Bank of England.

In the wake of the slump the exchange markets fell into disarray. World trade dropped, the economic depression proving so acute in countries such as Germany that political instability led to the rise of the Nazi dictatorship and drove the world back towards war.

The lessons of the gold standard

The gold standard system evolved over the centuries and was not a conscious or deliberate creation. Throughout the history of currencies one is left with the impression that governments moved in an *ad hoc* fashion from one expediency to the next. For the most part the learning process was slow, mistakes being repeated from generation to generation. The needs of the hour dictated change. Thus recoinages became inescapable. Credit control and interest rate management had to be adopted. Token coins and paper money became the norm through popular usage and demand. The gold coin was virtually abandoned as a circulating currency as commerce expanded. The expansion of domestic production throughout the world and the growth in international trade and commerce demanded international instruments of exchange, such as the letter of credit or bill of exchange, rather than mass movements of gold and silver.

Curiously, the reserve role of gold, although the cornerstone of the world's system, became completely over-shadowed by the use of sterling and, as the volume of international money transactions expanded, it became clear that the gold stock was in reality far too narrow for the efficient support of the money pyramid.

Technical change, too, was a potent force leading to change in the monetary system. The perennial problem of the debasement of the coinage was finally overcome by the adoption of the milled edge. Yet the need for recoinage was never overcome: even gold coins of the highest technical standard were subject to wear and loss of weight through constant circulation. In the commercial field, the displacement of sail by steam and of the mailcoach by the railway speeded up both the movement of goods and communications. The merchant and the banker were able to communicate across the world more rapidly. The telegraph, and later the telephone, led to a dramatic speed-up in communications, not least in the reporting of news which would affect business decisions.

All these changes influenced the development of the exchange system and the gold standard mechanism was adapted throughout that period of industrial expansion and technical change spanning the 200 years of the eighteenth and nineteenth centuries. For all its drawbacks, the gold standard system based on London served the developing industrial world well up to the First World War. It worked because the UK was the dominant country in the world's international transactions and the attempt to impose a stable value in the UK through a fixed and unchanging price for gold provided traders in other countries with a vehicle of exchange which could be accepted with confidence. Not only Britain's commercial supremacy, but her naval supremacy through the nineteenth century, contributed to international confidence in sterling. The important moral in this for the future of the world's reserve system is that it is natural for other countries to deal in the currency of the world's leading commercial and military power and to use that currency as the most common unit of exchange and as a reserve. A fall in confidence in that power and its currency results in an acute problem since the establishment of confidence in some other suitable unit can only happen gradually. It took two world wars to unsaddle sterling and the reserve role of the pound continued for another 60 years after 1914. Even today sterling still has a residual reserve role.

Since the worldwide acceptability of gold has never faltered, the interest in re-establishing some form of international gold standard is always significant. Wars and rumours of wars, revolutions and threats of revolutions have constantly led to a strong demand for gold as a store of value which can be taken from country to country in preference to paper currency. Governments, too, have been reluctant to eliminate gold from their portfolios of reserves. The question therefore arises whether a return to a gold standard is feasible. Perhaps the argument was best summed up by A. E. Feavearyear in his work *The Pound Sterling* referred to above. Writing just before the UK finally abandoned the gold standard in 1931, he identified its advantage as follows:

> For the second time we have returned to the gold standard because no other standard of which we have experience can give so near an approach to stability of value, and because so long as the majority of other countries favour gold it is the only way to secure stability of the foreign exchanges.

Since that date the world has had experience of a modified gold standard system under the aegis of the Bretton Woods agreement. We shall discuss this in a later chapter, examining the possibility of a return to such a system.

With regard to the disadvantages of the gold standard, Feavearyear went on to say:

> Failing, however, some new discovery of gold in the world, it behoves us, and all other countries, to economize the use of the metal. The accumulation of unnecessarily large reserves, ... besides being a waste of capital, is not in the interests of the world's production and trade; for the burden of fixed charges will inevitably hang as a heavier and heavier millstone round the necks of the producers as it did before the discovery of America, if there is to be a continuous scramble for gold[14].

Some 50 years later the scarcity of gold is an even more powerful argument against a return to the gold standard as it used to be. It must also be recognized that gold was not the perfect regulator it is sometimes claimed since the smallness of the gold reserves led to violent swings in commercial credit. The system was inoperable in wartime—but this would probably be true of any international exchange and reserve system. However, it must be recognized that economic management and the avoidance of extreme discomforts to millions of blameless people brought about by credit contraction and recession, required active central bank and government intervention in the credit and money markets to smooth the course of the gold standard.

Control of the money supply was never easy and it is a myth to suppose that there was an automatic regulator under the gold standard system. What the fixed price of gold achieved domestically was a rough and ready level of average commercial prices. The notion that prices were stable in Victorian England is

[14]FEAVEARYEAR, A. E. *The Pound Sterling*, p.327.

also a myth. Year to year fluctuations in prices could be sharp and this was certainly the case up to the 1870s. Erratic weather and harvests would drive food commodity prices up or down. The trade cycle, with its panics and crashes, would equally see industrial prices rising or falling sharply. Business management, in an age with scant intelligence in terms of national and international statistics, must have been approaching the impossible. The year to year fluctuations in prices, up and down, would have imposed huge problems with regard to stockholding and cash flow management was probably far more difficult than it has been since the 1930s, when prices have continued to change, but always in an upward direction.

Nevertheless, it is vital in any discussion of the future world system to examine the past for the evidence it holds of hard won experience. Society builds its knowledge painfully from experience and hands on that knowledge from generation to generation. Yet there have been instances in the history of the gold standard when the lessons of the past were either forgotten or overlooked. For this reason the record of the epoch of the gold standard based on London has a message for the future and we now examine the twilight period of sterling, following the First World War and the gradual emergence of the dollar standard.

2
The rise of the dollar

Expansion of the United States economy

The population of the United States surpassed that of the United Kingdom around 1870. With a steady inflow of migrants from Europe, population growth continued at a relatively fast rate in the US throughout the nineteenth century and the first half of the twentieth century. By contrast, there was a persistent outflow of population from the UK to the US, Canada, South Africa, Australia and New Zealand, reducing Britain's overall population growth. Between 1821 and 1932 over 18 million people emigrated from the British Isles and over 34 million immigrated into the US[1].

In parallel with population growth, US production of raw materials and manufactures expanded strongly, aided to a great extent up to 1914 by a considerable inflow of capital from the UK. US output in total surpassed that of the UK in the 1880s. In terms of shares of world industrial production, the UK was at her peak in 1870 with 32% compared with 23% in the US. The US share reached its peak in 1929 at 42%, by which time Britain's share had fallen to 9%[2].

In contrast to the UK, where industrial development had been financed by internal savings generated to a large extent by the revolution in agriculture, industrial expansion in the US depended heavily on foreign capital. Agricultural expansion in the US and the development of mineral resources resulted in virtual self-sufficiency so far as food and raw material supplies were concerned, and although exports of tobacco, cotton and grain were of large proportions, foreign trade was a small proportion of economic activity compared with the UK.

It was not until after the American Civil War that industrialization of the US economy began to rival that of the UK. The reconstruction period after the War resulted in a considerable boom. The resumption of farm exports contributed to the recovery. In many areas there was a shortage of skilled

[1]CARR-SAUNDERS, A.M. (1936). *World Population: Past Growth and Present Trends*, p.49. Oxford University Press.
[2]ROSTOW, W.W. (1978). *The World Economy, History and Prospects*, p.52. New York; Macmillan.

labour, resulting in high wage levels compared with Europe; this in turn gave an impetus to investment.

By 1914 the US had developed a vast steel industry and had achieved impressive economies of scale through mass production. She was thus poised to become the arsenal for Europe. While the European powers were weakening their productive capacity and ruining their international financial position, the US was able to transform its balance of payments and increase its share of world export markets.

Even so, the UK share of world trade was not overtaken by the US until the 1930s, in contrast to industrial output, where the US had overtaken the UK 50 years previously. The trade shares of the two countries are illustrated in *Chart 2.1*[3].

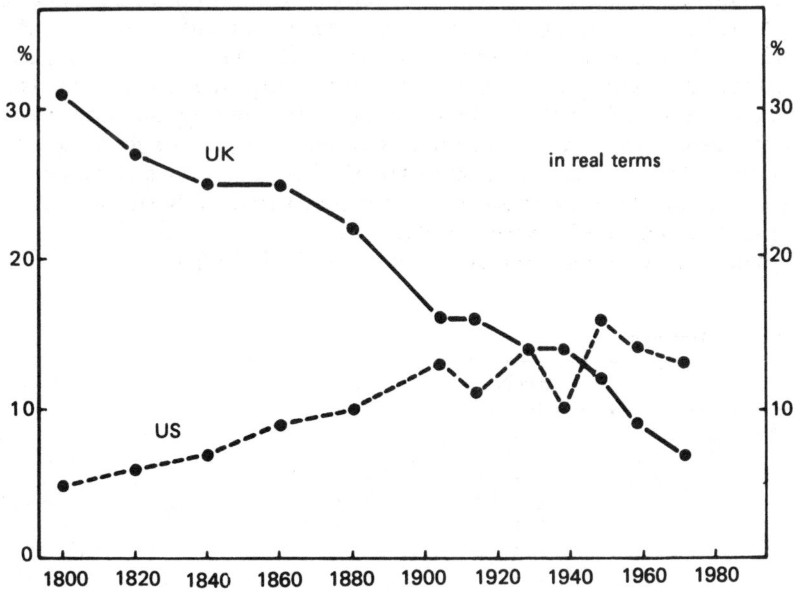

Chart 2.1 Shares of world trade

Thus in volume terms, the UK kept ahead of the US until the inter-war period and trade transactions in sterling remained greater, particularly because of the use of sterling in third country transactions. The figures expressed in volume terms are slightly misleading, however, due to relative fluctuations in prices and exchange rates.

It was also the case that the UK's transactions in invisibles—services such as banking, insurance and shipping and in remittances of dividends and interest—were in excess of those of the US. This position was also transformed to some extent with the First World War since US loans to Europe brought the US capital market onto the world stage and increased the importance of dollar transactions.

In total international transactions, therefore, the US began to edge the UK out of the first place during the First World War. The rise of the dollar dates

[3]ROSTOW, W.W. *The World Economy, History and Prospects*, pp. 70–73.

from that point. Even the 'great crash', dating from the end of 1929, failed to shake international confidence in the dollar. US banks failed in large numbers and the confidence of the American public was drastically affected. Yet the fact that US share prices fell by more than 70% between the peak of 1929 and the trough in 1932, and that production dropped by a half, was largely irrelevant so far as the balance of payments and the level of the gold reserves were concerned. If the slump had occurred in isolation, then world confidence in the dollar would have evaporated. As it was, the monetary systems in Europe were also badly shaken and the pound suffered more severely than the dollar, culminating in the sterling devaluation of 1931.

The US ran a surplus of exports over imports throughout the period of the recession. Even in 1932 the trade surplus amounted to nearly $300 million, so that the devaluation of the dollar in 1934, brought about by raising the price of gold from $20.67 per ounce to $35, led to the rapid accumulation of gold by the US in the subsequent decade. The US buying price of gold determined the world price and the devaluation of 1934 stimulated the production of gold. The new price was distinctly high in relation to the costs of mining and output was rapidly increased. Previously unremunerative mines were brought back into production and the purchase of gold by the US from other countries enabled the rest of the world to raise imports from the US to a relatively high level; this in turn perpetuated the US export surplus.

The changes in the US gold stock are illustrated in *Table 2.1*

Table 2.1 US gold reserves

	$ billion
1920	4.5
1929	5.0
1933	6.8
1939	17.6
1945	20.0
1949	24.4
1968	10.4

Source: US Treasury Bulletins, US Treasury Department

Between 1933 and the outbreak of the Second World War the gold reserve rose by nearly $11 billion and more than doubled. It rose to a peak of $24.4 billion in 1949, a vast total compared with other countries and in relation to US trade. At the pinnacle in 1949 the gold stock was equivalent to about six years' imports. At the same time, the UK's gold and foreign exchange reserves seldom exceeded the equivalent of three months' imports in the post-war period. By 1968 the US gold reserve had been so eroded by persistent payments deficits that it too covered no more than the equivalent of three months' imports.

Britain's preponderant share of world trade in the nineteenth century not only explains the dominant position of sterling in world markets and as a reserve currency but also the effectiveness of the gold standard based on London. The virtual absence of long-run price inflation in the UK, associated with the operation of the gold standard, ensured the acceptability of the role of sterling in the international monetary system.

That US trade never exceeded a 16% share of the world total, in contrast to a peak of 33% gained by UK trade, is not a true reflection of the rise of the dollar in world importance. For one thing, the growth in world trade was more rapid than ever before in the years after the Second World War and the value of trade transactions was boosted by a persistent rise in prices which was absent in the long period from 1815 to the 1930s. Perhaps more significantly, international capital transactions, in which the US was predominant, increased sharply from the First World War. The growth of the international industrial corporation, with subsidiaries in a number of other countries, was an important new feature of the world business scene and after 1945 the expansion of this form of international activity increased enormously.

In fact the rise of the dollar to replace sterling as the major international reserve currency was a slow and gradual process, spanning the whole of the inter-war period and sterling still continued as a major reserve currency after 1945.

The Sterling Area

As we have seen, the network of financial services centred on the City of London served a large part of the world up to the First World War, and that system operated on a relatively small gold reserve held by the Bank of England. After the War a large number of countries continued to link their currencies to sterling, maintaining balances by way of reserves in London. Those reserves were commonly held in the form of UK Treasury Bills which afford the advantage of virtually immediate liquidity as well as securing a modest rate of interest.

The system continued to offer the advantages of a greater degree of freedom of payments between the member countries than between them and non-sterling countries. The system was reinforced (or re-affirmed) in the wake of the world slump of the early 1930s. When Britain left the gold standard and devalued in 1931 many countries were confronted with a dilemma whether to following sterling or to keep their currencies stable in relation to gold and the dollar. A large number of countries, not only members of the British Commonwealth, followed sterling down and this resulted in the foundation of the Sterling Area.

The Commonwealth part of the membership of the Sterling Area gained cohesion with the signing of the Ottawa agreement in 1932 which created trade preferences between the members. In broad outline, the UK was allowed preferential entry for her goods to the other members of the Commonwealth while their goods enjoyed preferential entry in the UK. Tariff barriers were raised to outsiders and these 'preferences' contributed to a decline in world trade in the 1930s. In essence the UK gained preferential access to the markets of the primary producing countries of the Commonwealth for her manufactured goods in exchange for preferential entry to her own markets.

Thus the UK's 70-year exercise in free trade came to an end. The movement towards free trade had got under way in the 1840s and the British market was virtually free from tariff protection from the 1860s to the 1930s. Although it is argued that the UK's industrial growth suffered and that she lost markets, particularly since her rivals were developing home industry behind protective tariff barriers, trade centred on the UK was maintained at a high volume. Moreover, by importing cheap food—at the expense of home farming—the cost of living was kept low in the UK, helping to perpetuate cheap labour and so to retain export markets.

Although imperial preferences had been advocated by Joseph Chamberlain back in the nineteenth century, the abandonment of free trade was only adopted many years later. Similar long periods of debate and delay can be observed in British history over the abolition of the Corn Laws and the move from protectionism to free trade in the first half of the nineteenth century, and also with regard to collaboration with her European neighbours and entry to the European Economic Community (EEC). While the UK flirted with the idea of becoming a founder member of a new European order after 1945, opposition was only finally overcome and formal entry consummated with belated membership of the EEC in the 1970s—a delay of a whole generation. By that time the Sterling Area had withered away.

But in the 1930s the Sterling Area was a powerful trading bloc comprising roughly a quarter of the world's population. The system was more of a club than an official international agency, even if it had no formal rules. The member countries were 'expected' to base their currencies on sterling and to maintain the bulk of their reserves in London. For its part, the UK was 'expected' to manage its reserves in London on behalf of the members of the sterling club.

Whilst the system worked effectively in the 1930s, the seeds of its collapse were sown during the Second World War. As in the First World War, exchange control was exercised with a view to maintaining some semblance of stability and both in terms of the balance of payments and relative prices the pound was over-valued against the dollar. The UK again ran up substantial debts in her war financing in spite of the 'lend-lease' system with the US and her portfolio assets in the US were again put in pawn.

A notable feature was the accumulation of debt to other members of the Sterling Area. Instead of paying 'on the nail' for war costs incurred in India and Egypt, those countries extended credits in the form of sterling balances, so that at the end of the war the UK's liabilities to the Sterling Area, let alone her debts to the US, stood at exorbitant levels in relation to the central gold and foreign exchange reserve. Before the war the sterling reserves held in London by overseas countries amounted to over £470 million; against these the UK held reserves of £806 million. There was also additional cover in the form of short-term credits extended by British bankers throughout the world[4].

During the War the UK realized external assets to the value of £1118 million, increased her external liabilities by £2897 million and ran down her reserves by £152 million. The sterling balances rose from £476 million in 1939 to £3567 million in 1945, whereas the reserves declined from £802 million to £650 million[5]. The UK's reserves, on which the whole Sterling Area system rested, were only one-seventh of those of the US.

Under these circumstances it is a wonder that the sterling system continued to operate at all. However, the world shortage of dollars brought about by persistent US payments surpluses and the shortage of goods and materials,

[4]BAREAU, P. (1958). The Future of the Sterling System. *Institute of Economic Affairs, Readings*, p.7. London.
[5]Ibid. p.44 and p.52.

resulted in an overwhelming demand for dollars in the years of reconstruction following the war. Thus the established and orderly system represented by the Sterling Area retained its attractions for its members in a world where dollars were virtually rationed.

Indeed, the formation of the International Monetary Fund (IMF) provided a back-up reserve system which enabled the UK to limp along in maintaining the sterling system while the negotiation of a large line of credit from the US and Canada in 1946 was designed to help stabilize the position. A condition of the loan was that sterling was to be made freely convertible a year later—a sad error of judgement—for other countries immediately raided the sterling balances to obtain dollars, with the result that in August 1947 the UK had to ask the US for a waiver of this condition of the loan agreement. Sterling thus once more became an inconvertible currency.

An instructive feature of the 1947 crisis is that the cheap money policy in the UK, inaugurated in 1932, was still in force. With only a short exception at the outbreak of war, Bank Rate was pegged at 2%, a level maintained through thick and thin for nearly 20 years. Thus on the advent of convertibility in 1947, Bank Rate stood at 2% and the yield on three month Treasury bills was as low as ½%. No attempt was made, therefore, to hold funds in the UK by the expedient of higher interest rates: the argument being that a domestic deflation associated with a 'dear' money policy ran counter to recovery plans and the policy of full employment.

It has to be remembered that politicians were understandably obsessed with fears of a return to the conditions of mass unemployment of the 1920s and 1930s. Memories were long enough to recognize that the post-war money deflation of the 1920s brought about recession and very high unemployment. The return to the gold standard in 1925 reinforced the deflation and the financial turbulence of the 1930s slump drove unemployment still higher. Cheap money remained part of the economic plan to expand activity and to maintain a high level of employment after 1945. Hence there was a reluctance to pursue the logical policy of raising interest rates in support of sterling convertibility. Instead of a sharp and (hopefully) short adjustment, the UK bore the cross of an insupportable currency reserve role, with wholly inadequate reserves, for many years.

The demise of the Sterling Area

The post-war era was chequered with a series of sterling crises. Following the convertibility crisis of 1947, the payments problem forced a major devaluation in 1949. Further crises ensued in 1951, 1955, 1957 and 1961. Then from 1965 the UK seemed to live through a permanent sterling crisis, temporarily alleviated by devaluation in 1967 and mitigated occasionally in the 1970s as the dollar came under pressure.

The origins of the pressure on the pound lay first of all in the inadequacy of the central reserves held in London on which to operate the sterling system. As banker to the Sterling Area, the UK held far too little 'cash in the till' on which to support a world system. The short-term liabilities in the form of sterling balances which could be drawn down quickly and substantially by members of the system, were far too great in relation to those reserves. In 1951, for example, a major crisis developed as Sterling Area countries, which had quickly amassed large balances following the commodity price explosion on the outbreak of the Korean War, began to spend those balances. The war broke out in June 1950. Commodity prices soared and the foreign exchange earnings of countries such as Australia rose dramatically. The foreign exchange earnings of the members of the Sterling Area were automatically paid into London and their sterling balances in London increased correspondingly.

The first consequence was an impressive rise in the UK's foreign exchange reserves, so much so that the British government short-sightedly turned its back on US foreign aid under the Marshall Plan. That Plan, a truly marvellous feat of international generosity, provided substantial aid to the wartime allies of the US and also to the defeated nations to enable those countries to rebuild and rehabilitate their economies. Perhaps an act of enlightened self-interest, the scheme prevented the collapse of the economies of western Europe and the possible expansion of Russia's sphere of interest to the west.

Shortly after its inauguration however, the temporary improvement in Britain's international payments fortunes led the government of the day to declare that she could manage without further instalments of US aid under the recovery programme. Other countries were more prudent. In the event, as the foreign exchange earnings of the Sterling Area of 1950 were spent by the big earners in that area in 1951, the London reserves plummeted. The result was the imposition of a deflationary policy in the UK aimed, amongst other things, at correcting the balance of payments deficit and rebuilding the reserves.

By contrast, the previous crisis leading up to the large devaluation of 1949 was far less serious for the sterling system. The reason was that the pre-war exchange parities were hopelessly inappropriate in the post-war world. The dollar was heavily undervalued against most countries. Therefore the devaluation of the pound was a convenient signal to the majority of countries to make a matching devaluation against the dollar.

Nevertheless, throughout the 1950s, whilst the continental European and the Japanese economies embarked on an impressive recovery and expansion programme, the UK limped along with a far slower rate of economic growth. Growth rates exceeded an average of 5% per annum in the countries which banded together to form the Common Market. Unfettered by aspirations of world power, with low defence budgets, or virtually none at all in the case of Germany and Japan, a high proportion of national incomes was ploughed back into investment. The UK, on the other hand, retaining the mantle of a world power, spent far more on defence, took nothing by way of foreign aid and in consequence sapped her investment potential. Her plough-back rate was low, her expansion was slow and her ability to maintain her share of world trade and to achieve payments surpluses on which to sustain the Sterling Area banker role was inevitably sapped and destroyed.

The subsequent sterling crises form part of a long sequence of events marking the erosion of the UK as a world economic and military power and also as a financial power. An important contributory factor was the higher rate of cost and price inflation in the UK *vis-à-vis* the US and Germany. The rate of price inflation in the US and the UK throughout the twentieth century is illustrated in *Table 2.2*.

Although there were significant deviations, the long-run average rates of price change were broadly similar for the two economies up to the Second

Table 2.2 Prices in the twentieth century

Average annual rate of charge	*% per annum*	
	US	*UK*
1900–1914	2.1	1.1
1914–1920	8.3	16.8
1920–1929	-0.7	-3.7
1929–1933	-7.7	-2.9
1933–1939	1.6	1.5
1939–1948	6.9	6.7
1948–1952	2.3	5.0
1952–1968	1.6	2.9
1900–1968	2.3	2.7

Source: *The British Economy, Key Statistics*; London and Cambridge Economic Service

World War and to 1948. From that time the UK's price inflation has persistently exceeded that of the US, a feature which was certain in the long-run to create a preference for the dollar.

These problems created increasing difficulties in maintaining the cohesiveness of the Sterling Area. Moreover, the more rapid increase in output and trade of the non-sterling part of the world contributed to the relative decline in the use of sterling. The fact that sterling continued as a reserve currency, with governments and traders maintaining balances in London, owes a great deal to the strength of the City of London's financial institutions which developed during the UK's heyday in the nineteenth century. London's institutions and markets remained highly efficient. It was still possible in London to deal with speed, with confidence and with the minimum of formality. Hence the reserve role of sterling was maintained.

However, sterling was a long time a-dying as a reserve currency. In spite of the vicissitudes of the 1970s and the great run on the pound in 1976, which led to major restrictions on the use of sterling, the pound never disappeared completely from the list of internationally held reserves. By a queer quirk of fate falling confidence in the dollar was by then leading to attempts to diversify reserves out of dollars to some extent, so that within the period covered by the decline of sterling, the dollar climbed to its ascendancy and paradoxically began its own decline.

Instability of the inter-war period

The inter-war period was characterized by a degree of instability far greater than experienced under the gold standard up to 1914. Restrictions on international transactions were applied almost universally during the First World War and were never completely abandoned in the inter-war period.

At the outbreak of hostilities in 1914 conditions in the foreign exchange markets became chaotic. Oustanding contracts between the belligerent countries could not be honoured and the ban on trading with the enemy was more rigorously enforced than in any other period of hostilities. Enemy assets were seized and a moratorium declared on most foreign payments. In London gold exports were banned and gold arbitrage suspended from the outbreak of war so that the normal functioning of the exchange mechanism was interrupted. In addition, fluctuations in exchange rates were prevented at a later stage through official intervention by systematic 'pegging' operations. In neutral markets, however, exchange rates continued to fluctuate freely, thus providing some sort of guide to market forces.

Rates were 'unpegged' in 1919, leading to extremely erratic movements. The exchanges of the defeated countries slumped, being heavily undermined by rampant inflation. The currencies of the victorious European powers also declined against the dollar, reflecting the changes in economic fortunes brought about by the war. Speculation in currencies was at a high pitch, contributing to the exchange rate volatility. There was also a large volume of business in foreign notes which added to the instability of the exchanges. In 1920 the market in foreign bills at the Royal Exchange in London was closed down and from that point foreign exchange business was entirely concentrated in the foreign exchange departments of the banks and specialist brokers, operating via the telephone network. A forward exchange market evolved under the pressure of demand from commercial clients for facilities to cover exchange risks.

The period of floating exchange rates was brought to an end with the return of the UK to the gold standard in 1925. In the meantime, hyper-inflation in Germany had wiped out the value of the German currency and major international problems had arisen with regard to reparation payments and war debt.

It will be recognized that the turbulence of the international financial markets of the early 1920s was in sharp contrast to the relatively orderly conditions prevailing before the war. The shock of the war was immense in human terms and was reflected not only in economic change but in the political and social fabric of Europe. It is understandable, therefore, that in financial circles there was a powerful desire to return to the ordered systems of pre-war days and to re-establish the gold standard.

The period of stability was short-lived. For a while the international order was more settled and the UK, France and Germany drew together to some extent through the rapport established by Austen Chamberlain, Briand and Stresemann. The three countries struggled to recover from the effects of war, while boom conditions prevailed in the US. However, the Wall Street crash, the widespread contraction of credit that ensued in many countries and the resultant slump, had dire consequences in balance of payments terms. It also had a disastrous effect in raising unemployment to levels which threatened social upheaval and revolution.

The collapse of the Credit–Anstalt bank in Austria led to widespread banking problems in Germany. These culminated in a general moratorium which had repercussions for the UK. A large part of her acceptance credits were due to be paid by German businesses so that the moratorium meant that these foreign exchange assets were frozen. There was also a domestic crisis in the UK since the minority Labour government was unable to command confidence in its pursuit of a budget deficit. In brief, the crisis led to a run on the pound. Foreign deposits were withdrawn from London and even the raising of loans in excess of £100 million from the Federal Reserve and the Bank of France was insufficient to stem the outflow. Convertibility of the pound was suspended; the new government abandoned the gold standard and effectively devalued, letting the pound float once more. The fluctuations in the sterling/

dollar exchange rate in the inter-war period are illustrated below in *Chart 2.2* and *Table 2.3.*

Table 2.3 Sterling/dollar exchange rate (monthly averages)

	Highest (dollars)	*Lowest (dollars)*	*Range (cents)*
1919	4.77	3.80	97
1920	3.95	3.38	57
1921	4.17	3.63	54
1922	4.62	4.22	40
1923	4.70	4.36	34
1924	4.69	4.26	43
1925	4.86	4.77	9
1926	4.87	4.85	2
1927	4.88	4.85	3
1928	4.88	4.85	3
1929	4.88	4.85	3
1930	4.87	4.86	1
1931	4.87	3.37	150
1932	3.75	3.28	47
1933	5.14	3.37	177
1934	5.15	4.94	21
1935	4.97	4.78	19
1936	5.04	4.89	15
1937	5.00	4.89	11
1938	5.02	4.67	35
1939	4.69	4.03	66

Source: *The British Economy, Key Statistics*; London and Cambridge Economic Service

Thus the fluctuations between the monthly averages reached as much as $1.77 in the single year 1933 when the dollar approached devaluation; and the oscillation in the two periods of floating were, by any standards, severe.

From a low point in 1932, the recovery of the pound was substantial, threatening to undermine the export competitiveness gained by the UK by the 1931 devaluation. Accordingly, the British authorities intervened in the market, buying foreign currency and selling sterling in an attempt to hold down the rate. This led to the establishment of the Exchange Equalisation Account[6], set up by an office of the Treasury with the Bank of England operating the Account. The Bank of England was only permitted to buy gold at the official price, since the suspension of the gold standard had consisted only of relieving the Bank of its duty to convert bank notes into gold at par. Buying gold at the official price would not have held down the pound; hence the resort to acquiring foreign currencies was a novel feature having the effect of offsetting market forces to some extent and frustrating the rise in the pound.

Although this was no more than a move of expediency to meet a current problem, the Exchange Equalisation Account became a permanent feature of reserve and exchange rate management, its day to day operations being kept secret.

[6]HARROD, R.F. (1969). *Money*, pp.106–107. London; Macmillan.

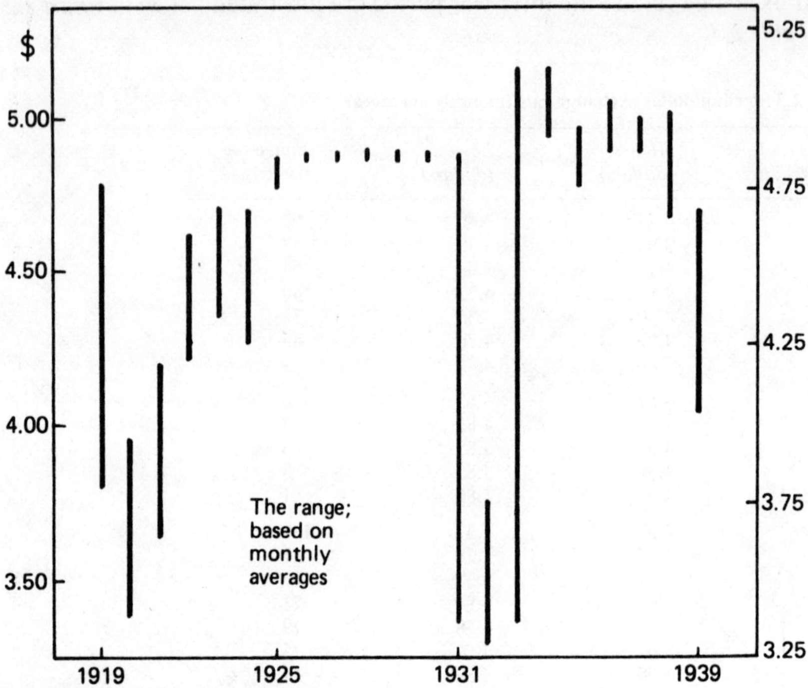

Chart 2.2 Sterling/dollar exchange rate

As can be seen from the exchange rate movements, conditions in the US had become equally unstable. After the war the US had adopted a tight money policy to prevent the large influx of gold leading to an inflationary credit expansion. The tenth annual report of the Federal Reserve in 1923 set out the main lines on which US monetary policy was to be conducted down to 1958[7]. This marked the end of the old semi-automatic gold standard. The quantity of money was to be regulated so as to even out the fluctuations in the business cycle (though the operators failed disastrously in the wake of the Wall Street crash) rather than to be fixed in relation to the inflows and outflows of gold. Domestic monetary policy was therefore divorced from external factors to a large extent a feature made possible by the vast official gold holdings and because of the relatively small dependence of the US on foreign trade.

The motive for the change was the desire to attain a stable level of prices and this ultimately contributed to the acceptability of the dollar as a universal reserve currency. It also stands out as an object lesson today so far as confidence, stability and the necessary characteristics of a reserve currency are concerned. In effect the US no longer adhered to a gold standard system as had been in force up to 1914.

A further important development of the early 1920s was the agreement reached at the Genoa Conference of 1922 not to re-issue gold coins on a return

[7]HARROD, R.F. *Money*, p.98.

to a gold standard. Having in mind the probable shortfall in gold production in relation to the potential expansion of commerce, international trade and money supply, governments were in effect requested to exclude gold from the currency circulation and were recommended to supplement reserve holdings of gold with foreign currencies. This subsequently became a permanent feature of international reserve management.

However, the mechanics of the world system of the 1920s proved flimsy in the face of the hurricane of the world slump. The problems of one country were quickly transmitted to problems for others and the decline in the pound from $4.86 under the gold standard to around $3.40 in 1931 put extreme pressure on the dollar. The pound was by then under-valued on purchasing power considerations, as can be seen from the fact that price movements in the two countries had averaged out at much the same rate since the turn of the century. The unemployment rate averaged 25% in the US in 1933 and it had peaked at 28% in the UK in the previous year. The employment position in the US was likely to deteriorate further with the dollar over-valued against the pound and other currencies as US producers lost market share.

Heavy speculative pressure on the dollar developed late in 1931 following the British devaluation. There were large withdrawals of foreign funds from the US as well as a flight of domestic capital[8]. This reduced the gold reserve and intensified the US banking crisis. Following his assumption of office in 1933, Roosevelt suspended the gold standard and freed the dollar to depreciate. The dollar fell to $5.26 at one point in November 1933 before speculative pressures were halted with the increase in the price of gold to $35 an ounce in January 1934.

This last move, however, switched the pressure on to the French franc and the currencies of the 'gold bloc' countries. France devalued, then Belgium in 1935, followed by Switzerland, Holland and Italy in 1936[9]. France devalued again in 1938, but by that time the threat of renewed war in Europe was leading to a flow of funds to the US. Europe's problems were worsening, leading to the complete ascendancy of the dollar.

Dollar ascendancy

It is impossible to grasp the degree of the dollar's ascendancy after 1945 without an appreciation of the strength of the US productive system in relation to the rest of the world. Devastation of productive assets was far greater in the Second World War than in the First. Once again the US had been the arsenal of the democracies and her productive capacity bounded ahead during the war. Not only that, the US did not suffer bombing and physical destruction. Her industries were elevated to a high pitch of capital intensity in comparison with the rest of the world. Her productivity per worker was far greater than any competing country. Her gold reserve was of massive proportions and, above all, the demand for her manufactured goods and commodities appeared to be insatiable.

[8]EINZIG, P. (1970). *The History of Foreign Exchange*, p.255. London; Macmillan.
[9]Ibid, p.256.

The productivity performance of the US appeared to be so far ahead of other countries that it seemed impossible that she could be overtaken. Other countries were only too ready to be able to acquire and hold dollars and it was logical that the Bretton Woods system should rest on the dollar. The IMF was the custodian of a modified gold standard system (discussed in the following chapter) under which currencies were linked via the dollar to gold.

As a result a persistent stream of US balance of payments deficits on current account supplied the world with dollars which it was anxious to hold as reserves. Moreover, the strength of the dollar, although restrained by the fixed exchange rate regime, contributed to the build-up of US industrial investment overseas. Since labour costs were so much lower in other countries, US corporations found it attractive to build up branches and subsidiaries abroad. This gave rise to a capital outflow similar to the outflow of investment capital from the UK prior to the First World War.

At the same time, the strength of the US economy attracted portfolio investment from Europe, where the narrowness of equity markets restricted investment opportunities at home for the large European investment institutions. In addition, the build-up of dollar reserves in other countries, as a direct result of the US payments deficits, led to purchases of US Treasury bills and short-term bonds by central banks. US liabilities increased at the same time as her ownership of long-term assets in the form of productive industrial investment increased, so that the international investment position of the US remained extremely firm. Confidence in the dollar was well justified.

By contrast, the fundamental weakness of sterling as a reserve currency persisted. The UK's share of world trade declined during the 1950's. The lost share in the protected markets of the Commonwealth and the recovering European and Japanese economies made large inroads into British trade. Britain's gold and foreign exchange reserves remained far too low in relation to the country's external liabilities; and low output and productivity growth, compared with other industrialized countries, meant that the significance of the UK economy in a world context continued to weaken.

Nevertheless, no other power was in a position to take on the role of a reserve currency. London's capital market was still far larger than that of any other European centre. Although Germany's foreign trade expanded rapidly, she ran a large deficit on invisibles account. She built up reserves rather than invest abroad. Japan, too, was bent on the rebuilding and expansion of her home economy. Thus the ascendancy built up by the US from the First World War reached a peak in the 1950s.

Neither was the infant IMF in a position to offer the world an alternative reserve system to the dollar. Indeed, the US dollar was made the cornerstone of the IMF exchange rate system, reflecting the immense size of the US gold stock at the end of the war and the universal confidence in the strength and stability of the US economy. Unlike most other trading nations, the US was to a large extent self-sufficient. She was a net exporter of food and agricultural materials. Her oil and mineral resources were vast. Her rich land mass was still far from fully exploited. She had a large and growing population. Her technology was foremost in the world. Her financial institutions were sound. Her inflation rate was low. Her labour force was highly skilled and productive and, in addition, the country had abundant self-confidence in its economic system and its dynamic qualities.

The US was thus uniquely placed to sustain the reserve role of the dollar in the post-war world. That pre-eminent position could have been maintained but for the mounting payments deficits of the 1960s associated with the Vietnam War and the consequent acceleration of price inflation.

The lessons of the transition period

The UK's domination of the world financial scene up to 1914 rested not only on her leadership in international commerce, but on the confidence generated by her own political and financial stability. Her ability to invest abroad added to that confidence and increased the use of sterling in world markets. In addition, price stability resulting from the operation of the gold standard increased the attractiveness of sterling as an international means of exchange and unit of account.

The confidence engendered by such a system enabled the UK authorities to operate with slender reserves of gold. By contrast, the rise in the dollar owed much to the great size of the US gold reserves. Confidence in the dollar rested on different factors; the inherent strength of the economy was based on abundant natural resources rather than the strength of US international trade. A common feature was the relatively stable purchasing power of the two currencies. Although price movements were erratic, the long-run rate of price inflation in the US was modest—at least by today's standards.

The decline of sterling was due in part to a faster rate of price inflation, but more particularly to the erosion of the UK's net international financial position. The outflow of capital from the UK was equivalent to some 7% of national product in the early years of the twentieth century[10] and her international balance sheet showed a large surplus of assets over liabilities. That balance sheet position was critically weakened in two world wars and her attempt to maintain a reserve currency role on a depleted asset base was probably doomed to failure. The fact that the UK had been able to sustain the gold standard system on a narrow gold base prior to 1914 may have misled her authorities into believing that the reserve system of the Sterling Area could be managed on a modest gold and foreign exchange reserve in the inter-war and post-war periods. In the event, the great imbalance between sterling liabilities, in the form of the sterling balances held by members of the sterling club, and the London reserves made the system vulnerable and unsustainable.

From the UK's point of view the sacrificies needed to protect the reserves and maintain the sterling system hampered her internal economy. Perhaps it is more accurate to say that the economic policies needed to raise British investment and productivity to the international average of her industrial rivals were missing and this must have contributed to the progressive decline of her international trading position and balance of payments. Even so, the reserve role would probably have been unsustainable in any case and other countries have been notably reluctant to let their currencies achieve reserve status.

[10]DEANE, P. and COLE, W.A. (1969). *British Economic Growth, 1868–1959*. Cambridge University Press; and *The British Economy, Key Statistics*. London and Cambridge Economic Service.

It is an illusion to think that anything approaching a stable system emerged after the abandonment of the old automatic gold standard as it had operated up to 1914. It was recognized in the inter-war period that gold supplies would not be adequate to support the old-style gold standard and foreign currencies were introduced into the reserve system. That the dollar was able to fill this role so successfully after the Second World War was due to the strength of the US economy, political and financial stability, and a low rate of price inflation. These are indispensable features for a modern reserve currency and we now turn to see how the dollar fulfilled that requirement under the Bretton Woods system.

3
The Bretton Woods system

Reaction to the 1930s

In the western democracies discussions began during the Second World War about the problems of the pre-war world and the kind of structures needed to overcome those problems once the war had been won. Not only was there concern about mechanisms for maintaining peace and an appraisal of the League of Nations to learn from its shortcomings, but there was equal concern about the economic roots of war and the collapse of the economic order in the 1930s. There was particular concern about the mass unemployment of the inter-war period and the excesses of the swings in the business cycle. Not least, there was concern at the erratic behaviour of the foreign exchanges, the weakness of the international monetary system and the decline in world trade.

High and persistent levels of unemployment were not, of course, a unique feature of the 1930s. At all times from the Middle Ages unemployment has been a feature of society and in retrospect it would seem the era of full employment in the industrial economies after the Second World War was unique. Yet the severity of unemployment was so acute in the 1930s that there was great public and political concern to find a solution and build that solution into the post-war reconstruction settlement. War has a revolutionary impact and creates the opportunity for the kind of structural change achieved in peacetime only by laborious efforts over long periods. Thus the opportunity arose in 1945 to adopt new systems, because a common will existed for change and the need for reconstruction was so great.

A feature of the 1930s had been the contraction of world trade following the financial collapse leading to the slump. Widespread bank failures in the US, followed by chronic international payments problems, led to the abandonment of the gold standard by the UK and a series of exchange rate devaluations. The motives for the devaluations were more than attempts to restore a favourable balance of payments, although in the case of the UK in 1931 this was imperative. Another reason was the attempt to stimulate exports and to keep out imports in order to encourage home industry at the expense of foreign competition. It was hoped thereby to create more home employment and thus to curb unemployment.

This 'beggar my neighbour' policy was virtually doomed to failure, for its immediate effect was to reduce international trade and thereby to remove a stimulus to industrial activity. Instead of helping to reduce unemployment, such policies pursued by the leading trading nations only served to worsen unemployment in the world as a whole. In Britain's case the abandonment of free trade, which had contributed to the successful expansion of world trade up to 1914, under the operation of the gold standard system based on London and the foundation of the Sterling Area with its system of imperial preferences, helped insulate her from the worst effects of the economic blizzard. At the same time the abandonment of free trade contributed still further to the contraction of world trade and the mass unemployment problem.

The need was, therefore, to establish an international payments and exchange system aimed at preventing deflationary downward spirals, as had occurred with the 1930s slump, and to foster the expansion of international trade.

Proposals for reform

Rival schemes were canvassed by the US and the UK and the drafts were published in 1943. The origins of these proposals for reform were laid down in 1941 in the Atlantic Charter drawn up by Roosevelt and Churchill. This spelled out the aims of the two democracies for a better world order, including economic opportunity for all peoples. In the same year a scheme was devised to assist the UK in her war effort at a time when her balance of payments had virtually exhausted her capacity to buy essential materials and armaments from the US. The 'Lend Lease' scheme circumvented Congressional legislation which banned money loans to belligerents. The problem of returning the items loaned (an impossible proposition) was met by drafting a 'Mutual Aid Agreement' under which the UK committed herself to co-operating with the US in establishing a better economic order in the post-war world.

Article 7 of the Agreement prescribed an endeavour to reduce obstacles to international trade and to eliminate discriminations. The US Secretary of State, Cordell Hull, was a persistently strong advocate of freedom of trade, though whatever Britain's sympathies with such an objective, her prospective post-war balance of payments problems and the existing system of imperial preferences made it nearly impossible for her to comply. Confronted with such objectives and problems, Keynes on the British side devised a scheme providing for an increase in international reserves sufficient to create a breathing space in which countries could make the adjustments which would ultimately pave the way for freer trade.

While Keynes began work on his proposals in 1941, Messrs White and Bernstein of the US Treasury also began work on proposals for an International Stabilization Fund, without knowing that Keynes was engaged on a similar project in London. The two plans were published and discussed and became the subject of an important conference between the US, Britain and Canada in Washington in September 1943. This was followed by a wider conference in 1944 at Bretton Woods, where it was agreed to establish both the International Monetary Fund (IMF) and the International Bank for Reconstruction and Development (IBRD).

The individual 'Plans' are worth considering today since the background problems of the 1930s were similar in many respects to the background problems of the 1970s. Keynes' radical approach and fertile imagination led him to propose a system providing for modest adjustments in exchange parities under the supervision of an international board. In common with the White plan, Keynes proposed the adoption of an international unit of account, a new form of money representing a certain weight of gold, to be used exclusively by governments or central banks for the settlement of international debts.

The White plan envisaged what amounted to a return to the gold standard[1]. It advocated the creation of an international unit of account to be called 'Unitas' with a gold equivalent of 137½ grains and equivalent to ten US dollars. In addition, each national currency was to represent a fixed weight of gold and in consequence to have a fixed value in terms of unitas. The new unitas reserve asset was to be established by a body known as the United Nations Stabilization Fund. The plan also envisaged that each country which joined the Stabilization Fund would 'maintain by appropriate action the exchange rates established by the Fund on the currencies of other countries'. This rigid approach implied that a stable exchange regime, which presumably offered the promise of long-run price stability, would be maintained by adjusting internal economic forces by varying both credit and fiscal policies. The objections to the plan logically focused on the near monopoly by the US of the world's gold holdings and the problem of determining appropriate and sustainable exchange rates in a world economy hugely distorted both by the events of the 1930s and the war itself.

The Keynes plan appeared to be more realistic in that it allowed for the immediate imbalances of the post-war period. It proposed to leave it to each state to fix the initial value of its currency, in agreement with other members, in terms of a unit to be called 'Bancor'. In common with the White plan, the new reserve unit was to be fixed in terms of gold and to relate each national currency to bancor. However, unlike the White plan, Keynes envisaged that parities would be adjusted from time to time to accord with changed internal conditions. Such changes would have reflected relative movements in costs and prices and in the balance of payments. Specifically, an alteration in parity would only be permitted where the country in question had been in substantial balance of payments deficit for a period of two years, and the permitted change in the exchange rate would be no greater than 5%. This would only be allowed once and any further adjustments would need the assent of the governing body of the new fund or clearing union.

A provision was also made that during the first five years of operation of the new system the governing body would be empowered to give special consideration to requests for an exchange rate adjustment on the ground of unforeseen circumstances. It was assumed that thereafter alterations in parities would be rare; in other words, in the light of experience following the First World War, it was foreseen that a five year period of trial and error and adjustment in rates would be required to usher in a new era of relative stability.

Both schemes thus provided for a return to some form of gold standard. Recognizing the maldistribution of official holdings of gold and the likelihood that supplies of gold would only increase slowly, a revolutionary unit of account

[1]COLE, G.D.H. (1944). *Money, Its Present and Future.* London; Cassell. For a contemporary account of the debate written in 1943, see Chapter 14.

was proposed, with countries depositing gold in the new fund. The fund would then have a backing for the new currency unit and would be able to extend credits to member countries. The British scheme went further than the American in this respect. In effect an international bank would be established, providing a facility for the expansion of international liquidity and world trade. Although differing in detail, the two schemes were in broad agreement on these points.

The need for a new international reserve unit to supplement gold can be seen from the distribution of gold holdings on the outbreak of war (see *Table 3.1*). The US held nearly 60% of the world's official gold, excluding Russia and, at the time of the discussions on the Keynes and White schemes, it was generally agreed that the US share would be even greater at the end of the war.

Table 3.1 Gold reserves as at June 1939

	US $ millions
United States	16 110
France	2 570
United Kingdom	1 067
Netherlands	800
Belgium	668
Switzerland	599
Argentine	428
Sweden	346
India	274
South Africa	219
Canada	213
Italy	194
Japan	164
Roumania	138
Norway	107
World (excluding USSR)	24 942
Exchange Equalization Funds	2 300
Total	27 242

Source: *Money; Its Present and Future,* by G.D.H. Cole

So far as gold production was concerned, output in 1939 was valued at $1383 million, of which South Africa accounted for a third and Russia nearly 13%. Of the total only part was available to boost monetary reserves and newly mined gold probably represented no more than a 2% increment to the stock of monetary gold.

The Bretton Woods agreement

It should be borne in mind that the discussions regarding monetary reform took place in wartime when many other pressing problems impinged upon the time of the advisers and decision-takers. It was also the case that only a few countries could be consulted and represented adequately. When agreement was reached at Bretton Woods in 1944 to set up the IMF, a large number of the countries participating were represented by expatriate governments. Nevertheless, since perfect solutions were never likely to be reached and compromises had to be made, it was probably more important to allow the momentum of wartime energy and will to agree and reform, and so to carry the nations concerned to a relatively quick agreement.

The structure proposed by the US was accepted by the British with some misgivings. The British plan had proposed, like the American plan, that countries would be able to draw upon the Fund up to amounts agreed upon in advance. But in the British plan the ability of the Fund to honour those drawing rights would have rested upon the willingness of creditor countries (which inevitably meant the US in the short run at least), to accept claims upon the Fund as a final discharge of indebtedness. When a country drew out of the Fund, it would thus reduce its own claim upon the Fund, while the recipient country—the creditor—would increase its claim. By contrast, under the US proposal the Fund would simply meet the drawings through members having initially made subscriptions, or deposits, in gold and in their own currencies. The Americans were frightened at the possibility of what appeared to be an open-ended commitment to meet the drawing rights of all other members and they logically foresaw that such a proposition would not pass the US Congress.

The possibility, therefore, had to be considered that the Fund would find it impossible to honour the drawing rights of members if those members were preponderently in debit with the US on balance of payments. This difficulty was met by a shrewd proposal which ultimately became Article 7 of the IMF Agreement, namely the 'scarce currency' clause. This laid down that:

> ...if it becomes evident to the Fund that the demand for a member's currency seriously threatens the Fund's ability to supply that currency, the Fund shall formally declare such currency scarce and shall thenceforth apportion its existing and accruing supply of the scarce currency with due regard to the relative needs of members.

The supply of a member's currency to the Fund would, of course, have been limited by the amount of the member's original subscription. The article went on to say:

> ...such a formal declaration shall operate as an authorization to any member, after consultation with the Fund, temporarily to impose limitations on the freedom of exchange operations in this scarce currency.... The member shall have complete jurisdiction in determining the nature of such limitations, but they shall be no more restrictive than is necessary to limit the demand for the scarce currency to the supply held by, or accruing to, the member in question...[2].

By implication, the authors were inferring that there would be continuing exchange controls and that currencies would in general be inconvertible. This somewhat blinkered view was at odds with the very concept of the Fund, which envisaged that all members would make their currencies convertible as soon as possible. Such are the pitfalls of compromise. In a world of convertible

[2]HARROD, R.F. *Money*, p.272.

currencies there would be no reason for any particular member to hold a specific amount of the 'scarce' currency.

In effect, the authors appear to be looking backwards to the 1930s in permitting countries to discriminate against the 'scarce' currency country with presumably a strong balance of payments. In a sense this form of restriction was at odds with the whole concept of the IMF as laid down elsewhere in its articles. The Fund is in fact an agency of the United Nations, reporting to the Economic and Social Council of the UN and was established:

> ...to facilitate the expansion and balanced growth of international trade, and to contribute thereby to the promotion and maintenance of high levels of employment and real income and to the development of the productive resources of all members as primary objectives of economic policy...to promote exchange stability...and to provide countries 'with opportunity to correct maladjustments' in their balance of payments without resorting to measures destructive of national or international prosperity.

Such broad aims could be interpreted as allowing members to pursue their own priorities and generally to avoid deflationary policies. It could be presumed that the pursuit of exchange rate stability implied a regime of price stability and monetary restraint, as attributed to a gold standard system. In practice, there was a conflict of interests.

The agreement provided that members must avoid exchange restrictions and maintain a stable exchange rate by intervening in the market to prevent rates moving by more than 1% away from the agreed parity. This entailed buying foreign exchange when the rate approached the upper limit, thus adding to the reserves, and selling foreign currency from the reserve to support the rate when it fell towards the bottom end of the range of permitted fluctuation. The 2% bands thus approximated to virtual exchange rate stability and in practice rates were maintained within slightly narrower bands.

The Fund is owned by and administered on behalf of member governments, in contrast to the Bank of International Settlements (BIS) which is an organization run by the central banks. The central banks, however, are closely involved in the operation of the IMF and many countries appoint their central bank governor as their governor for the Fund. The governors for each country are the ultimate controlling body for the Fund. They exercise votes in accordance with a formula weighted by 2% of national income in the year 1940, 5% of gold and dollar holdings as at 1 July 1943, 10% of average annual imports in the base period 1934–1938, 10% of the maximum variation of annual exports in the same period, the sum of these items being increased by the ratio of average annual exports to national income in the 1934–1938 period. This formula was slightly biased in favour of the smaller members, though this was of little consequence since on matters of substance changes had to be approved by every member having more than 10% of the voting power. This meant that the US and the UK were granted an effective veto[3]. The basic decisions reserved to the governors covered a general revision of quotas, a rise in the world price of gold and a change in the Articles of Agreement.

[3]HIRSCH, F. (1969). *Money International.* Harmondsworth; Penguin Books. Chapter 13 contains an outline of the IMF system.

Although Russia took part in the original discussions she did not become a member and Poland and Czechoslovakia withdrew in 1950 and 1954. Neither did Switzerland become a member, and New Zealand did not join until 1961. Thus, although having an extremely wide membership, the absence of Russia in particular prevented the Fund from exercising a truly world role.

There is an annual meeting of the governors of the Fund which has become a valuable meeting place as well as a general forum for bankers and finance ministers. The meeting is synchronized with the annual meeting of the World Bank, the new name for the International Bank for Reconstruction and Development.

The voting formula was also used to determine members' drawing rights. The initial quotas, or deposits, were made up of approximately one quarter in gold and the balance in the member's currency paid in special non-interest-bearing notes. On making a drawing from the Fund, the member purchases foreign currencies from the Fund for a further payment made in its own currency. Drawings can be made automatically in foreign currencies to the extent of the member's gold quota and in this sense countries can regard the gold quota as part of their own directly controlled reserves. Nevertheless, drawings of this part of the quota still have to be repaid. The Articles of Agreement set an initial limit on drawings of 25% of quota a year, but this limitation was modified in the 1950s. A drawing covering an additional 25% of quota has generally been made available by the Fund without 'strings' provided that the Fund is satisfied that the country in question is making an effort to deal with its payments problem. Beyond that, however, the Fund requires 'substantial justification' for larger drawings and these are subject to a rising degree of scrutiny of the member's economic policy. The normal limit of drawings is the point where the Fund's holdings of the member's currency reaches 200% of quota. Since the Fund would have held 75% of the member's quota in its own currency in the first place, the drawings limit therefore amounts to 125% of quota. The articles specify no time limit for drawings.

A service charge of ½% is made on purchases of a currency, and drawings beyond the limit of the gold tranche are subject to a scale of charges rising with the size and length of borrowing. These range from 2–3½%, with a top marginal rate of 5%—remarkably cheap money. Repayments can be made in gold or an eligible convertible currency where the Fund's holdings are less than 75% of quota—that is, a Fund creditor's currency.

With regard to exchange rate parities, the Agreement stipulated that members had the right in effect to change the par value by up to 10% unilaterally, but on one occasion only. Any further adjustment beyond 10% was not permitted without the agreement of the Fund and for this the correction had to be to deal with a 'fundamental disequilibrium', a state of affairs which was not defined. The par values were, of course, fixed in terms of gold and for convenience expressed in terms of the US dollar. Thus, with the US owning a vast stock of gold and the price firmly fixed at $35 per ounce, the virtual certainty of the US maintaining a balance of payments surplus in the immediate post-war period and the rest of the world tending towards payments deficit, the scene was set for the world to embark on a dollar standard when the IMF opened its doors for business in 1947.

The US dollar had become a reserve currency *par excellence*.

Bretton Woods in operation

As was discussed in the previous chapter, the UK was ill-equipped to sustain the role of world currency in the aftermath of war. The Sterling Area was not sustainable given the UK's large sterling liabilities and international debts on such an inadequate base of gold and foreign currency reserves. After the fleeting experiment with convertibility in 1947, when the US loan facility was speedily exhausted, it quickly became apparent that the initial exchange parities established after the war were unrealistic and unsustainable. Thus, when the UK devalued from $4.03 to $2.80 to the pound in 1949 many other countries took the opportunity to make a matching adjustment. On a purchasing power parity the pound was fixed at too low a rate, though the damage to the UK's overall terms of trade was reduced by the simultaneous devaluation of many of her trading partners.

Having used up the initial 'unquestioned' devaluation limit allowed under the rules of the IMF, exchange rate adjustments for many countries could from that point only be made with the concurrence of the Fund. That the world exchange system functioned relatively smoothly into the 1960s must be attributed to the remarkable generosity of the US in launching the Marshall Plan. Inaugurated by the Secretary of State, George Marshall, the scheme recognized the great imbalance between the strength of the US economy and the impoverished state of the war-ravaged European and Japanese economies. A massive programme of aid was set in train, partly with the object of rebuilding Europe as a bulwark against the spread of communism. The immense sum of $20 billion was dispensed over a period of years, achieving something which the IMF and the World Bank could never have accomplished, and leaving the IMF to deal with more temporary and adjustable payments problems between members.

During the 1950s reconstruction continued apace in Europe. Trade barriers were reduced. The General Agreement on Tariffs and Trade (GATT) had been established, allowing import restrictions only as a last resort and imposing a ban on export subsidies. It provided a forum for the orderly reduction of tariff barriers, and the gradual reduction of import duties contributed to the fast growth of international trade. The establishment of the European Free Trade Area and the European Economic Community also fostered a rapid expansion of trade within Europe with a marked effect continuing through the 1960s. In addition, economic co-operation was co-ordinated to some extent through an organization set up to administer US aid and this subsequently became the Organization for Economic Aid and Development (OECD)[4].

These stimuli resulted in the most rapid phase of output and trade growth in the world's history. From the beginnings of the US aid programme in 1948 to the world oil crisis in 1973, world output growth averaged more than 4% per annum in real terms, while trade expanded at twice that pace. Export growth and investment growth were the engines of expansion and, with hindsight, cheap energy, particularly oil, also contributed to industrial expansion. Between 1953 and 1973 output growth of the OECD group of countries

[4]The Organization for European Economic Co-operation was established in Paris in 1948 to administer the Marshall Plan in Europe. It was transformed to the OECD in the 1960s with the US, Canada and Japan as additional members.

averaged 4½% per annum with the Communist bloc not far behind. From 1960 to 1973 the economies of the OECD expanded by as much as 5¾% per annum, reflecting the contribution of accelerating trade within the newly formed Common Market in Europe.

Output and productivity growth in Europe and Japan were faster than in the US with the consequence that the competitive edge of the US was gradually blunted. Other countries' share of world trade in manufactures improved and during the 1950s the US balance of payments surplus gave way to persistent, though modest, deficits. In effect the US pursued a truly 'good neighbour' policy, the Marshall Aid scheme putting other countries in funds and enabling them to follow expansionist policies regardless of their underlying payments deficits in the earlier years. Indeed, some recipients were able to build up foreign currency reserves from the proceeds of the Aid scheme.

By the second half of the 1950s the payments position of other countries had so far improved that the long delayed move to currency convertibility, as envisaged under the IMF Agreement, could be implemented. As early as 1950 the European Payments Union (EPU) was established as an agency of the OECC as a financial clearing arrangement which cut through the network of bilateral payments agreements between the European countries. Through the EPU member countries could offset debits and credits in other inconvertible member currencies. Net settlements could then be made with the EPU partly in gold and partly in credit. The BIS acted as the operating agent for the EPU, thereby gaining valuable experience in further co-ordinating the international dealings of the central banks.

At the end of 1958 the countries of western Europe allowed their currencies to become generally convertible under the European Monetary Agreement. Under this arrangement the members were to notify each other of the buying and selling rates they proposed to maintain in spot dealings against the US dollar. This move had been helped by a 50% increase in IMF quotas, a relatively modest change in relation to the growth in world trade and transactions.

In the meantime the IMF's facilities had been widely used, 92% of the drawings in the first ten years being in US dollars. These drawings thus reduced the Fund's holdings of dollars to 28% of the US quota in 1957. This gave the US a gold tranche position with the Fund of nearly $2 billion, a useful supplement to her domestic gold and foreign exchange reserve[5]. Thus far the Bretton Woods system had worked well and confidence in the dollar still stood at a high level, in spite of persistent US payments deficits.

Those deficits had served to reduce the US gold stock from a peak of $24 billion in 1949 to around $21 billion in 1958. But, as is shown in *Table 3.2*, the rate of decline then accelerated until a rock bottom figure of $10 billion was reached in 1971. This level was regarded as a virtually irreducible minimum and necessary as a strategic reserve.

Up to the mid 1960s the US holdings of foreign exchange were relatively modest, amounting to no more than $1.7 billion in 1966. Those holdings rose to nearly $5 billion in 1969, then falling to no more than $2 billion in 1971. Thus the persistence of the US payments deficits and their increase during the course of the Vietnam War were reflected in an embarrassing decline in total reserves.

[5]HIRSCH, F. *Money International*. p.364.

Initially this presented no particular problems for the IMF since arrangements were made through a stand-by credit with the Fund enabling the US to draw eligible 'creditor' currencies from the Fund, coinciding with repayments to the Fund by countries holding mainly dollars in their reserves.

Table 3.2 US official gold reserves

	$ billion
1945	20.1
1949	24.4
1958	20.6
1963	15.6
1968	10.9
1971	10.2

Source: US Treasury Bulletins, US Treasury Department

In the meantime, having overcome the payments crisis of 1957, the UK was again in difficulties in 1960, making it likely that she would once more apply for a drawing from the Fund in 1961. By that time the great post-war dollar shortage had evaporated and the position reversed; the possibility also arose of the US herself being obliged to apply for a drawing from the Fund. The deutschemark was now the scarce currency and under a strict interpretation of the articles of the Fund it would have been possible for the mark to have been declared 'scarce' and for other countries to have taken discriminatory measures against Germany.

Such a step does not appear to have been considered and a way round the potential problem was devised by Per Jacobsson, the Managing Director of the Fund, by persuading ten leading members of the Fund to enter into stand-by loan agreements to the Fund. The agreement, known as the General Agreement to Borrow (GAB), was subsequently ratified, the ten partners—the US, Canada, UK, France, Germany, Italy, the Netherlands, Belgium–Luxembourg, Sweden and Japan—being known since as the 'Group of Ten'. The total stand-by credit amounted to $6 billion and was first used by the UK in 1964, and again in 1965 and 1967, and by France in 1968. The facilities were not unconditional but were supplementary to the IMF system rather than an increase in the Fund's direct facilities and authority.

The need to proceed to the extent of creating an additional mutual loan network also illustrates the failure to increase world reserves up to that point in line with the rapid growth in world trade. Whereas reserves were equivalent to around one year's imports before the Second World War, by 1963 the reserve ratio was down to 45%. A key factor was, of course, the unchanged price of gold, regardless of world inflation since its fixing in 1934. Roughly no more than half of newly-mined gold found its way into official reserves, so that the adequate build-up of reserves rested heavily upon the acquisition of reserve currencies. With the decline in the Sterling Area system and with a negligible supply of hard currencies such as the deutschemark and the Swiss franc for use as potential reserves, the reserve role had fallen increasingly upon the dollar. The need to maintain full confidence in the dollar was, therefore, of still greater importance.

Another significant development of the early 1960s arose from events in 1961. As a result of intense speculative pressures, the deutschemark was re-valued upwards by 5%, a move followed by the Netherlands. It was widely held that the German revision was too small and that France, Italy and Switzerland would also follow the upward revision. A new wave of speculation set in and there were heavy withdrawals from London and switching into Switzerland in particular. The switching route was via the US dollar, putting the dollar under strain in spite of the neutral characteristics of the manoeuvre. In the wake of this feverish bout of currency speculation, the central bankers met in Basle for their routine monthly gathering and issued a statement at the end of the meeting asserting that they were co-operating closely in the exchange markets. The aim of the operation, as described in the Bank of England's Quarterly Bulletin (September 1961, p. 10), was that 'No party to the so-called Basle Agreement should be forced by speculative movement of funds to deviate from the declared policy'.

Movements of capital, or 'hot money', of a destabilizing nature to the exchanges were thus officially frowned upon and from that point mechanics were evolved for reversing such flows through 'swap' agreements. If a country received a speculative inflow of funds, the resulting balances would be re-lent back again to the country of origin or else held by the receiving central bank without conversion so as to keep pressure off the exchange rate of the country of exodus. The arrangement was aimed initially to help the UK but it was subsequently widened to form part of a defensive network for the dollar. By 1965 the US had built up swap lines with eleven central banks, as well as with the BIS.

What was significant was that these expedient steps were taken outside the IMF system. In conjunction with the Group of Ten arrangements, the Basle facilities look in retrospect like a vote of no confidence in the Bretton Woods scheme of things. Governments and central banks had opted for *ad hoc* arrangements to deal with current and growing problems rather than to reform and expand the Bretton Woods system. A practical reason for this preference probably lay in the difficulties in the way of achieving major changes in the IMF system arising from the Fund's large membership and somewhat complex rules. Even so, the IMF facilities remained a vital part of the international monetary system and members have continued to make substantial drawings on those facilities.

The decline of the Bretton Woods system

The decline of the Bretton Woods system can be traced throughout the post-war period. Indeed, it can be argued that the system was never fully implemented. Nevertheless, exchange rate adjustments were fairly orderly until other pressures undermined the whole fabric of the managed exchange rate system. That system rested critically upon confidence in the dollar and the gold link. Once the gold parity of the dollar and other currencies was threatened, the days of the managed exchange rate were numbered.

The fact that the Group of Ten was brought into being and that the network of swap arrangements was developed to help stabilize the exchanges, was a reflection of the growing inadequacy of the Bretton Woods system. Or perhaps it would be fairer to say that it was not so much the Bretton Woods Agreement as the failure of politicians and bankers to operate that Agreement which led to the breakdown of the system. By the late 1950s, the rapid growth in world output and trade, the scale of Marshall Aid and the cumulative impact of the modest US balance of payments deficits were still manageable problems so far as the world monetary system was concerned. Yet those problems were not mastered and were reflected in two features. The first was the uncontrolled development of the Eurodollar markets, and the second was the failure to adjust the gold price in an orderly fashion and in such a way as to maintain confidence in the gold–currency link.

The origins and growth of the Eurocurrency markets were symptomatic of the growth of international business and banking. They were also a reflection of the imbalance in the world monetary system stemming from the progressive build-up of the US balance of payments deficits. This subject is explored in more detail in the following chapter.

But a greater threat to the Bretton Woods exchange rate regime was posed by the difficulties in maintaining the price of gold. Throughout the 1950s the price of gold in the London market fluctuated within fine limits around the official US dealing price of $35 per ounce. There was very little private speculation so that the proportion of new gold going into official reserves increased to some extent.

From 1958, however, things changed. Dollar shortages had given way to a brief period of balance and from 1958 more and more dollars began to accumulate outside the US. Since most of these found their way into official reserves, other central banks were in a position to demand gold from the US for dollars. Hence the US gold stock began to decline at a faster rate and outside observers could assess the continuing payments deficits, the decline in the gold stock and the steady erosion of the value of money through price inflation, and draw the inference that sooner or later the price of gold would be forced up. Apart from the argument that the shortage of officially held gold in relation to the expansion of world commerce would require an increase in the gold price to raise the value of gold reserves and restore an adequate level of international liquidity, a decline in confidence in the value of money with persistent inflation was an argument for the private investor to acquire gold as an inflation hedge.

During 1960 speculative pressures began to develop and the US authorities were warned of the growing demand for gold. By late October the London price had been forced up to $40, in effect establishing a two-tier market. To neutralize speculative demand required heavy sales from the US gold stock and close collaboration between New York and London to restore and hold the price at $35. This led, later in 1961, to the setting up of the international gold pool to spread the burden between central banks of selling gold for dollars in order to hold the gold price at its official level. Nevertheless, the arrangement provided no more than a cushion for the US gold stock since there was no obligation for the European authorities to hold dollars permanently in the place of gold. It was still legitimate to convert official dollar holdings into gold by means of purchases from the US authorities.

This loose arrangement proved effective enough for a number of years, although there were increasing warnings, notably from the British economist, Sir Roy Harrod, of a potential shortage of world liquidity and of the need to raise the official gold price. In the event, the devaluation of the pound from

$2.80 to $2.40 in November 1967, sparked off a large wave of speculative buying of gold. It was argued that the US payments deficits were relatively greater than the UK deficits, that the UK devaluation would lead to a further worsening of the US payments position, and that the dollar would need to be devalued; in other words, the official price of gold would have to be raised. Following a heavy drain on the US gold reserves, the operations of the gold pool were suspended in March 1968. By then France had dropped out of the pool arrangements and the remaining six members agreed that they would continue to remit gold at the old price of $35 per ounce to other central banks in exchange for their own currencies, but would no longer contribute to the gold pool. This virtually insulated the existing official gold holdings from the market and the open market price then settled permanently above $40. A two-tier market had become a permanent feature, undermining the original Bretton Woods concept of a gold/exchange parity system.

At the same time, the social upheavals in France brought about by the May riots in Paris resulted in highly inflationary wage settlements and, later in the year, speculative pressures built up against the French franc. There was a powerful movement out of francs into the deutschemark, accompanied by switching from sterling to marks. An emergency meeting of the Group of Ten was summoned late in November but, rather than re-value, Germany initiated a reduction in her border taxes on imports and rebates on exports, imposed a 100% reserve requirement on any additional foreign deposits with German banks, as well as a positive restriction on foreign deposits. This amounted to a restriction on capital movements and a departure from the basic principle of currency convertibility on the part of a country which had pursued open and liberal policies. It should also be noted that these changes were not accomplished through the direct mechanisms of the IMF.

No doubt the erosion of the Bretton Woods gold/exchange system was accelerated by the policy stance adopted by France. Following the devaluations of the franc in 1956 and 1958, the Gaullist regime exercised a strong preference for gold. In discussions on the reform of the reserve system during the 1960s. France was consistent in her advocacy of a stronger role for gold and for a higher gold price. There was also a powerful logic in preferring gold to dollars in an era when what could be regarded as irresponsible US payments deficits served to flood the world with dollars. France was herself forced to devalue by 11% in 1969 and, in spite of a general increase in reserves by the issue of Special Drawing Rights (SDRs) in 1970 and subsequent years, the Bretton Woods exchange rate system finally collapsed. First the US abandoned convertibility of dollars into gold in August 1971, breaking the key link so far as the IMF parity sytem was concerned. The subsequent attempt to stabilize the exchanges, resulting in the Smithsonian Agreement, failed to halt speculative pressures and the open market price of gold continued to rise. The official gold price was raised to $38 per ounce in 1972, well below the open market price, and the US then made a second devaluation early in 1973.

In the wake of the US move away from gold in 1971 the IMF governors asked the executive board of the Fund (twenty of its financial officials—the Group of Twenty) to prepare a detailed scheme of reform and to report on the kind of body needed to make detailed recommendations on the shape of the new system. The Group of Ten also began informal discussions to find an agreed pattern of exchange rates as a temporary basis pending a more permanent arrangement. These exploratory talks culminated in the ministerial meeting at the Smithsonian Institute in Washington in December 1971 agreeing a new set of exchange rates. Sterling and the French franc were maintained at their existing parities against the SDR while other currencies were adjusted both up and down.

This did not amount to a return to the fixed regime of the Bretton Woods system. There was no acceptance of convertibility and, with the US having abandoned gold and with negligible holdings of foreign exchange, she was powerless to defend the dollar parity unless other countries intervened in the exchanges by way of support. In addition, wider margins of fluctuation in exchange rates were accepted, the bands being widened to 2¼% either side of the agreed central parities.

The nature of the 'revolution' and abandonment of the Bretton Woods system can be seen from the adoption of the SDR as the *numéraire* in place of gold, the adjustment of the dollar's parity (whereas it had been the fixed star in the exchange rate firmament) and the multilateral realignment of currencies.

Floating exchange rates

From that point (December 1971) exchange rates have been allowed to fluctuate by wide margins. The movement towards a freely floating exchange rate system has been hesitant, governments and central banks continuing to intervene in the markets both to smooth out daily movements and to check extreme market movements. We have therefore experienced a 'dirty' rather than a 'clean' float in the exchange markets and the fluctuations have been somewhat less than in the 1930s.

Even so, the inconvenience of the fluctuations arising from the dirty float has been sufficient to maintain pressure from traders for a return to a more orderly system of exchange parities. The possibility of wide exchange rate movements has raised the costs of international trade while uncertainty over future prices has inhibited trade to some extent.

Flexible exchange rates have also had a market impact on price structures through relative changes in import and export prices. With a weak currency import prices have risen faster, imparting an additional element of cost inflation to the domestic economy. It has also cheapened exports, tending to increase export opportunities. In this sense flexible rates can be seen as offering a means of correcting a balance of payments deficit although unless they are accompanied by internal measures to half price inflation, the higher cost of imports may serve to maintain the inflation disparity between countries. The converse also applies and what we have seen in the 1970s is a tendency for the strong to get stronger and the weak weaker. The low inflation countries have experienced strong exchange rates which have helped to keep down price inflation, while the high inflation countries have tended towards weak exchange rates, perpetuating their higher rates of inflation.

Although freely floating exchange rates, without government and central bank intervention in the exchange markets, thus reducing the need to hold reserves of gold and foreign currency, is a plausible method of managing national economies, the associated discipline of non-intervention in the domestic economy has not been followed and appears to be quite unacceptable in the modern political economy. For this reason it seems inappropriate to consider the development of such a system as a probable outcome in the future. The lessons of the Bretton Woods system point out the failures of the way in which that system was operated but do little to confirm that a floating exchange rate regime offers a lasting solution to the world's monetary problems.

The lessons of the Bretton Woods system

It must be acknowledged that the Bretton Woods system had served the needs of the hour in the immediate post-war period. The modified gold standard system provided for members to make adjustments to correct payments imbalances while avoiding major deflationary episodes damaging world trade. Fixed exchange rates provided a stable background for trade in contrast to the volatile swings of the floating regime of the 1930s.

The system was undermined from three directions; first from the escalating payments deficits of the US, gradually flooding the world with ultimately unwanted dollars; secondly, from the advent of the Euromoney markets which were themselves a by-product of the US payments deficits; and finally, from accelerating price inflation at disparate rates between the major trading countries.

The system withstood the problems arising from the gradual demise of sterling as a reserve currency. It also provided the necessary forum for bringing ministers, bankers and officials together at many levels to establish *ad hoc* arrangements for dealing with international monetary problems. It is also significant that when speculative pressures and massive movements of short-term capital overturned the system, the contacts and mechanics built up over the years enabled the major trading nations to continue to search for *ad hoc* arrangements to deal with the growing problems. Systems evolve under the stimulus of market forces and the development of a floating exchange rate discipline has taken place in the tortuous environment of record peacetime price inflation and a dramatic rise in oil and energy prices.

In considering the future of the dollar and the world reserve systems it is vital to explore the possible outcome of the world energy crisis and the prospects for inflation. But we first turn to examine the origins and growth of the Euromoney markets and the consequences for the international monetary system.

4

The rise of the Euromoney markets

The origins of the market

The Eurodollar market has been defined by the BIS as the acquisition of dollars by banks located outside the US. This came about through the taking of deposits designated in dollars and to some extent through exchanging other currencies into dollars and the re-lending of those dollars.

The origins of the market are sometimes credited to the Russians. Fears of the possible blocking of Russian-owned dollar balances in the US led to the holding of those balances in London and the lending of dollars outside the US. This was in 1957. However, the return to currency convertibility in 1958 by the major members of the IMF paved the way for the expansion of international capital transactions. By itself convertibility was not a particularly powerful motive for the development of an offshore international capital market, and the real motivating force was the restriction on interest payments imposed on the US banking system.

Regulation Q limited in a particularly severe way the rate of interest US banks could pay on deposit. No interest was allowable on deposits for less than 30 days; no more than 1% could be paid on time deposits of between 30 and 90 days; and there was also a maximum rate of 2½% on time deposits of between 90 days and six months. At that time, the dollar was still an extremely hard currency and in relatively short supply since the US payments deficits had been modest through the 1950s. The US rate of price inflation was low, contributing to the attractiveness of the dollar as an international unit of account.

While US deposit rates were at an unrealistically low level, bank lending rates were at a high level with a wide margin between the two. This margin was sufficiently wide to allow London banks to seize the opportunity to attract business away from the US. As the Bank of England described the development in 1964:

> Banks in London have been able to attract large sums in dollars by quoting better rates for deposits, including interest on money at call and short notice—categories which earn nothing at all with New York—and have employed them at less than the US lending rate and still made a worthwhile turn. They are able to operate on a fairly small profit margin because the

additional overhead expenses of conducting their Eurodollar activities are minimal[1].

As it was, continuing US balance of payments deficits provided a steady stream of dollars, part of which could be utilized by the London market in providing a new international facility.

Full credit must be given to the ingenuity of the bankers in developing the system. Not only that, it must be recognized that the international banking system operated from London from the nineteenth century onwards remained extremely efficient, facilitating rapid deals with a high degree of confidence. Because of the worldwide trading and banking links of the City of London, many foreign banks maintained branches in London and then, as now, more banks were represented in London than in any other centre in the world.

From its beginnings in the late 1950s, the growth of the market was remarkable, not that the techniques were unique. Einzig[2] points out there was a thriving business in sterling and dollar deposits based in Berlin and Vienna during the inter-war years, an extension of the mediaeval practice of drawing bills payable at the quarterly fairs in terms of currencies other than those of the countries of payment. International trade in foreign currencies has existed for as long as trade between nations, so that the principles of the Eurodollar market are not a new innovation but are based upon a long history of borrowing and lending in foreign currencies. Yet the Eurodollar market was different in the specialized nature of the transactions and their size.

The term 'market' sometimes causes confusion because of our general familiarity with markets in a physical sense. A cattle market or a street market is a place where buyers and sellers come together. Stock exchange and commodity markets have a similar characteristic, the difference being that although the specialist traders meet at specific locations to conduct a market, their customers place orders and instructions in the main by telephone to the dealers. But the foreign exchange markets and the Eurocurrency markets are 'telephone' markets; that is to say, there is no physical meeting place which constitutes a market but rather a network of dealing offices interconnected by telephone and telex. Prices and rates are transmitted this way and deals struck, reflecting the most favourable terms matching buyers and sellers at any point in time.

The term 'Eurodollar' market is also misleading. As the market developed, expatriate funds of other countries in other currencies were mobilized and business expanded in other centres, notably Paris. But the origin of the market clearly lay in the growing flow of dollars to the outside world and the interest rate differential between New York and London.

The growth of the market

Although regulation Q was amended to permit the payment of higher rates of interest at various times during the 1960s, the Eurocurrency market expanded apace. Apart from the effects of the curbs on interest in the US in driving funds out (or keeping them out), on the other side of the Atlantic bank rate had been

[1]*Quarterly Bulletin, Bank of England*, (June 1964).
[2]EINZIG, P. (1970). *The Eurodollar System*. London; Macmillan.

raised in 1957 to the then crisis level of 7%. After the crisis subsided, interest rates in London remained firmly in excess of those ruling in New York, creating a permanent opportunity for matching lenders and borrowers to their mutual advantage via London and other European centres. Convertibility now made it possible to convert out of dollars into the currency of the countries where investment was to be made or goods to be purchased, if these were outside the dollar area.

In this connection, a major force behind the growth of the new international capital market was the rise in importance of the multinational corporation. Although international companies, either with wide trading links or branches and subsidiaries in other countries were a well established feature—some like the Hudson's Bay Company with a very long history—their expansion into a world economic force dates from the 1950s. The International Telephone and Telegraph Corporation (ITT) was a relatively small domestic US corporation in the early 1950s; by the 1970s it had become one of the largest corporations in the world.

Apart from the giant oil companies, the US motor companies, chemical companies, durable producers, electrical companies, machinery manufacturers, food corporations and so on, straddle the free world economy with production units or branches in a growing number of other countries. Although on a far more modest scale, other advanced countries (notably the UK) had expanding corporations ranking with the US multinationals. With the rapid increase in world trade, international business was increasingly dominated by the multinationals, particularly the US corporations. Thus with a hearty appetite for capital to finance foreign investment, the Eurocurrency markets provided a source of funds to supplement retained cash flow. The market grew to meet a need.

The raw material for the initial take-off of the market was provided by the US payments deficits. Some idea of the growth of the dollar outflow can be gained from the chart showing US gold and foreign currency reserves and US liabilities to foreigners. By 1960 liabilities exceeded reserves. By 1970 liabilities exceeded reserves by over $30 billion—a ratio of over three to one. By 1977 the ratio had risen to ten to one, with an excess of liabilities over reserves of more than $170 billion. This development is shown in *Chart 4.1*.

The liabilities arose, of course, from the payments deficits. Apart from three years, the US remained in overall payments deficit continuously from 1950 to 1980. Although of little consequence in the 1950s, from 1958, the year of convertibility, to 1978 the payments deficits reached an aggregate of nearly $160 billion. In the later phases of the Vietnam War, the deficits reached truly alarming proportions, exceeding $20 billion in 1972.

Part of these dollar outflows found their way directly into the official reserves of other countries, the larger part indirectly through commerce and the foreign exchange markets. While rates were pegged under the Bretton Woods system and the dollar firmly tied to gold, central banks were virtually compelled to absorb the dollar outflows. But in the natural course of business, dollar balances were increasing in the world banking system outside the US, thus providing the raw material for the international capital markets.

Neither did US restrictions on the outflow of capital halt the development of the market. In 1963, the US introduced the Interest Equalization Tax, designed to erode the interest rate differentials in favour of other centres, and

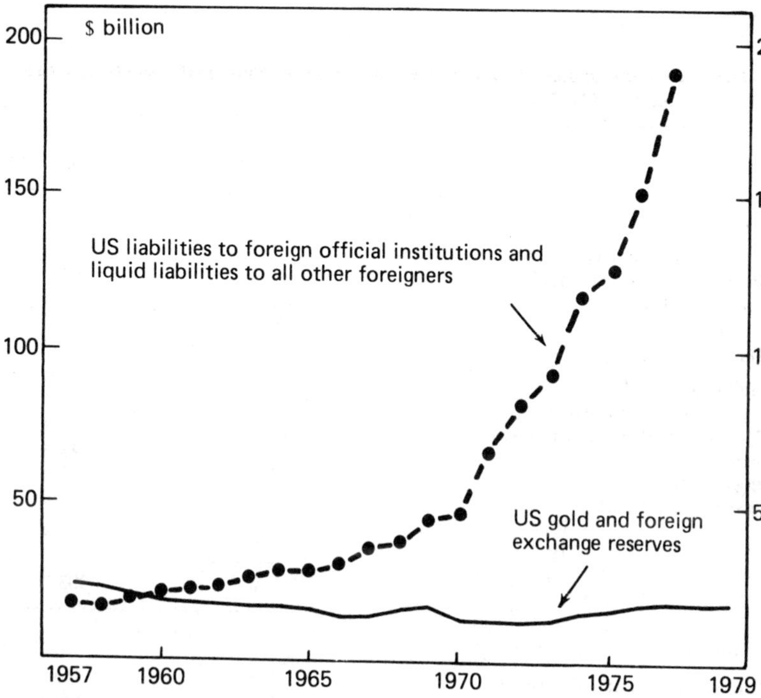

Chart 4.1 US reserves and liabilities

in 1965 Foreign Credit Restraint Guidelines were published, voluntary at first and then mandatory, aimed at curbing the outflow and coupled with controls over the direct investment abroad of US corporations. These restrictions had the inevitable effect of driving dollar business away from the US markets and contributed to the remarkable growth of US banking business in London, to the point where more American banks were represented in London than in New York. In fact, there are now more than 200 foreign banks operating in London, by far the largest number of any international banking centre.

The basis of the market is the deposit of funds with banks situated outside the countries from which those funds originated and for which those countries are responsible in terms of bank controls. For every 'offshore' deposit there has to be a counterpart. Often there is a chain of 're-depositors', but at the end of the line there has to be a deposit with a bank in the country of the currency's origin. For example, an export from, say, France to the US, may result in the dollar proceeds being invested with a London bank. There will thus be a counterpart to the London deposit with the US bank through which the payment was made. The transaction may be more complex than this and give rise to multiple counting of the funds in question; but after 'netting out', the simple relationship between the domestic US currency and the Eurocurrency remains.

A further reason for the growth of business outside the US is the restriction on branch banking. US banking corporations are not permitted to operate national branch networks and are restricted to their home states within the

Table 4.1 External positions, in domestic and foreign currencies, of banks in the reporting area and of certain offshore branches of US banks[1]

	($ billion) Dec. 1976	Dec. 1978
Banks' claims on		
Group of Ten countries and Switzerland	269.5	472.7
of which Reporting European area[2]	192.7	362.8
United States	33.3	53.0
Canada	9.4	17.9
Japan	34.1	39.0
Offshore banking centres[3]	83.5	123.8
Other countries in western Europe	42.7	50.7
Australia, New Zealand and South Africa	11.8	13.8
Eastern Europe	28.8	47.6
Oil-exporting countries	24.1	57.2
Non-oil-exporting countries[4]	80.9	123.4
Unallocated[5]	6.1	13.8
Total	547.4	903.0
Banks' liabilities to		
Group of Ten countries and Switzerland	319.6	539.3
of which Reporting European area[2]	240.5	409.5
United States	56.3	102.1
Canada	12.6	15.8
Japan	10.2	11.9
Offshore banking centres[3]	56.0	97.1
Other countries in western Europe	32.6	35.8
Australia, New Zealand and South Africa	2.4	2.7
Eastern Europe	7.6	10.7
Oil-exporting countries	64.2	83.8
Non-oil-developing countries[4]	49.8	78.0
Unallocated[5]	11.3	17.0
Total	543.5	864.4

Source: Bank for International Settlements: Annual Report No. 49, Basle, June 1979
Note: The figures in this table are based partly on estimates.
[1]The offshore branches of US banks, whose external positions are included in the figures, are those located in the Bahamas, Cayman Islands, Panama, Hong Kong and Singapore.
[2]Up to 1 December 1977 the reporting European area covered Belgium–Luxembourg, France, Germany, Italy, the Netherlands, Sweden, Switzerland and the UK. Since 1 December 1977 it also includes Austria, Denmark and Ireland. Conversely, as from 1 December 1977 positions vis à vis Austria, Denmark and Ireland are excluded from the positions vis à vis 'Other developed countries'.
[3]Bahamas, Barbados, Bermuda, Cayman Islands, Hong Kong, Lebanon, Liberia, Netherlands Antilles, New Hebrides, Panama, Singapore, other British West Indies.
[4]Including those countries in the Caribbean area which cannot be considered as offshore banking centres.
[5]Including international institutions.

Federation. It has therefore been in the interest of the major US banks to seek business abroad where the domestic restrictions do not apply. Under these influences the range of currencies in which the market operates has continued to widen over the years and the number of centres participating in the market has gone on increasing.

So far as the size of the market is concerned, there are obviously problems of measurement and definition because of the number of countries involved, and the inclusion of the same deposit in the deposit levels of a number of different countries. The statistics are monitored by the BIS and its annual reports give detailed accounts of the progress of the market. The main expansion of the market dates from 1964. By the end of 1978 the external assets of the European reporting banks had reached $500 million in foreign currencies; approximately two-thirds of the total were in dollars.

The geographical composition of the market as a whole is illustrated in *Chart 4.1.*

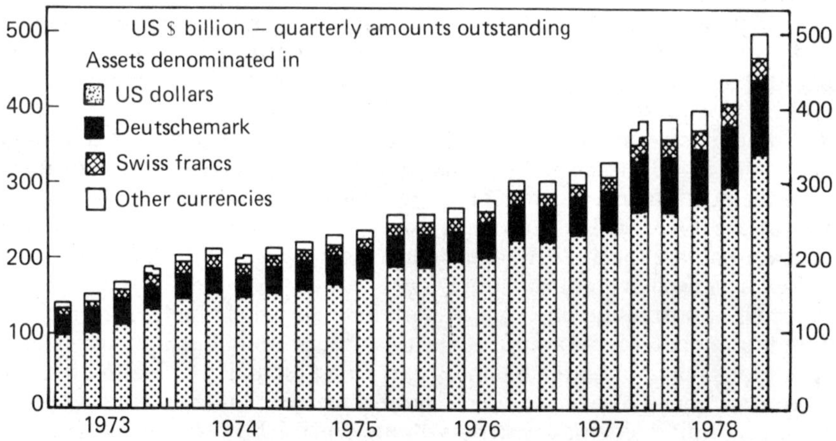

Chart 4.2 Currency structure of the Euromarket: external assets in foreign currencies of reporting European banks. (Source: Bank for International Settlements, Annual Report No. 49, Basle, 1979)

It will be seen there was a heavy expansion from a total of liabilities from $543 to $864 billion between the end of 1976 and the end of 1978, an increase of nearly 60%. The currency composition and growth of the market from 1973 is illustrated in *Chart 4.2.* The question arises of how such an increase can occur and how far it contributed to the accelerating rate of price inflation in 1979–1980. Moreover, the present scale of the market is out of all proportion to the cumulative US payments deficits and indicates clearly the drawing in of funds from other countries. What is disturbing is the possibility of a credit multiplier at work in the Eurocurrency markets, inflating world money supply, regardless of the central bank controls of the various domestic monetary systems.

The Eurocurrency system

The Euromarket has grown to the point where it is far more important than the

IMF as a source of funds to the world economy. Total drawings on the IMF in 1979 amounted to around $4 billion, whereas international bond issues through the Euromarket exceeded that level in the first quarter of 1979 alone. In 1977, the total of issues exceeded $19 billion. What has happened, therefore, is that while progress has been retarded at the official level in developing, or reforming, or replacing the Bretton Woods system by the difficulties in securing agreements between sovereign national states within the international community, private self-interest of the giant banking and commercial organizations has succeeded in creating a massive world capital market to meet the needs of the hour. That market has survived attempts to curb it, has coped with the problems of the move to floating exchange rates, and has provided a vehicle for the recycling of funds arising from the redistribution of income and capital following the oil price explosion.

To a large extent the market is an interbank or wholesale market. Transactions are usually of the range of $1 million or more. The lending is principally between banks en route to a non-bank borrower. This entails a considerable degree of trust in that the chain of intermediaries may be uncertain of the origin and destination of the funds in question. Yet the participation of such a wide range of banks ensures the smooth operation of the market, optimizing the return on the funds and spreading risk.

The market is essentially short-term, as distinct from the domestic equity and government bond markets. Deposits tend to be for short-term maturities, suiting the portfolio management requirements of the participating banks and corporations. Over 90% of Eurobank assets are for maturities of less than one year; over half are for three months or less. Borrowing and lending are closely matched by length of maturity.

Another important function of the market is to provide a hedging facility for the multinational corporations against exchange rate fluctuations. Those corporations may hold large balances in the market and are able to diversify between currencies or switch either to protect their capital or in some instances to secure a profit. Hedging operations of this kind can be destabilizing if part of a generalized move from one currency to another and will be regarded by central banks and governments as speculation. No doubt the market facilitated large movements of funds and brought added pressure on various currencies from time to time through the 1960s and 1970s. Flights of funds from sterling and the dollar, inflows into Swiss francs and deutschemarks as well as other permutations may well have accelerated the swings in exchange rates and even forced governments to take offsetting action. Indeed, extreme movements have contributed to major shifts in domestic economic policies and have contributed to the unpopularity with some commentators and politicians of both the Eurocurrency system and the floating regime.

In addition, central banks have participated in the market, securing higher rates of interest than have been obtainable in the US domestic market on reserve holdings. These transactions have been of substantial proportions on occasions and redepositing of funds in this way has led to claims that money supply growth has been expanded in an irresponsible way. Since 1971, however, the major central banks have agreed not to utilize the market; by contrast developing countries have been heavy users of the market. Whereas loans from the IMF intended to help deficit countries through a period of balance of payments adjustment have been restrictive, imposing deflationary policies on the borrower, no such restraints apply to loans raised in the Eurocurrency markets. The higher rates of interest entailed have not generally acted as a deterrent.

The impact of these transactions on international liquidity is important. When, as a result of a US payments deficit, private markets have an excess of dollars, the surplus is presented to the central bank for conversion into the local domestic currency. If the central bank then reinvests those dollars back into the private markets the excess supply of dollars is resurrected and the process continues, thus tending towards money creation. Where central banks both lend and borrow directly from the market, the surplus country acquires assets backed by the liabilities of the deficit country, thereby adding to the reserves of the creditor country. Yet the borrowings of the deficit country are not considered to have depleted its official reserves so that the operation can be said to have added to international liquidity.

Thus, although central banks intervene in the Eurocurrency market, the market as such is not subject to regular controls and guarantees as is the case with domestic systems. There is no lender of last resort and no automatic procedures for protecting a country against sudden and large movements of funds. Countries have, of course, collaborated in attempting to neutralize, or moderate, large movements and the network of swap and support arrangements between central banks has been mobilized from time to time to help stabilize the exchange markets.

Credit creation and inflation

The very size and rate of expansion of the Eurocurrency market raises the question whether credit creation through that market has served to create money and to contribute to world price inflation. The theory that 'every advance creates its own deposit' is virtually a law of domestic banking. The user of bank credit facilities draws cheques which then pass into other deposits, thus raising the lending capacity of the receiving banks. Assuming opportunities exist for profitable lending, part of the new deposits not subject to the conventional reserve ratio will be lent out in a continuing sequence until the point is reached where the original credit increase has been matched by new deposits. In other words, the growth of bank credit is equivalent to a direct increase in the money supply.

This is the case for the domestic banking system and control of the system rests with the central bank of the country concerned. Every deposit arising in the banking system of that country will be subject to the reserve requirements and regulations of the day. Since operations in the Eurocurrency market amount to the transfer of funds from one country to another, the levels of bank deposits in the two countries are adjusted and the funds still remain under the control of the domestic central banks concerned. In theory, therefore, the operations of the Eurocurrency market cannot be held responsible for credit creation.

This point of view has been put forcibly by Bareau[3] as follows:

[3]BAREAU, P. (1979). The International Money and Capital Markets, *Institute of Economic Affairs, Readings 19*, London.

> The theory has been advanced by eminent economists that the Eurocurrency float or pool is simply the product of the commercial banks' mystic power to create credit—not, it is true, out of nothing, but out of a comparatively small reserve base of liquid assets.
>
> I entirely reject this explanation. I cannot believe that a chain of Euro-banks can create, shall we say, dollars independently of the wishes or policies of the Federal Reserve authorities. It is out of the question that, for example, a French and a German bank can by their bilateral, or multilateral, operations create sterling outside the volition of the Bank of England.

The argument appears convincing but will only be true if the central banks in question really do have control (and exercise that control effectively) over their entire domestic banking systems. The evidence of the 20-year period during which the Eurocurrency market has blossomed and bloomed suggests that central bank control has been far from rigorous in the majority of countries and that the banks operating the international market have been able to generate inflationary credit expansions in the domestic markets.

This was the view of Friedman, writing in 1969[4], and Harrod also leaned to the view that the Euromarket facilitated credit creation. Looking at the requirements of the end-borrowers, Harrod made these observations[5]:

> When the borrowed dollars are used to pay debts denominated in dollars, there does not seem to be a possibility of any such creation.

In other words, such a transaction may be regarded as a matching transaction in a domestic country's banking system. But he contrasted this with the kind of transaction where the international market is used not to obtain funds in another currency but to obtain funds from that source in preference to the local market. The example was cited of British local authorities borrowing heavily in the Eurodollar market because it was the cheapest source of short-term funds. The dollars were not required and the borrowers probably never saw the dollars. Dollars borrowed by this class of borrower are likely to go back into the Eurodollar circuit.

Harrod went on to conclude:

> If I am correct in this, the quantity of dollars for *end-uses* i.e. excluding mere bank to bank re-lending, exceeds the number of dollars initially placed in the market, provided that some of the borrowers are operating in the same way as the Local Authorities referred to in the example.

The apparent uncertainties and disagreements between authorities over the question of credit creation arise because of practical difficulties in exercising control over domestic banking systems rather than from any flaw in banking theory. The hard fact is that the world's banking system has found an escape route from domestic controls and restrictions and has sought a higher level of profit through the development and growth of a complex and sophisticated international short-term capital market.

An examination of the mechanics of a Eurocurrency transaction illustrates the possibilities of credit creation. Eurodollars come into existence when the

[4]FRIEDMAN, M. (1969). *The Eurodollar Market: Some First Principles*. Morgan Guarantee Survey.

[5]HARROD, R.F. *Money*, pp.324–326.

owner of a deposit with a US bank transfers the title to that deposit to a bank based abroad. He then has a dollar claim on the foreign bank and the foreign bank has a claim on the New York bank. At this point a Eurodollar is an indirect way of holding a deposit with a US bank. But when the foreign bank starts to lend its Eurodollar assets the position alters. If the dollars lent by the foreign bank are redeposited in that country, then Eurodollar liabilities in that country will no longer be matched in full by claims in New York. By making loans and taking deposits, banks in the foreign country can create Eurodollars in excess of the deposits held in New York. Yet somewhere in the system there must be deposits in New York, since it is by shifting the title of funds in New York that transfers of funds are made. However, the degree of credit expansion (the multiplier effect) will be far more modest than with the conventional reserve and lending ratios operating in purely domestic banking markets[6].

It must be concluded, therefore, that the wide disparity between the size of the cumulative US payments deficits since 1950 and the ultimate size of the Eurocurrency market as a whole, reflects some degree of credit creation through the mechanics and use of the market and the absence of universally effective control over the domestic banking systems on the part of the central banks. As we have seen, the BIS itself has not been blameless in this respect.

With regard to the activities of the Eurocurrency market and the expansion of credit, the 1979 Annual Report of the BIS has this to say:

> Apart from its impact on private liquidity, the vast US official settlements deficit boosted, of course, world official exchange reserves. Although the current account surpluses were heavily concentrated in a few industrial countries that invest their exchange reserves predominantly in the US financial markets, international bank lending helped to share out the reserve accruals to countries that generally deposit a large part of their reserves in the Euromarket. In this way international bank lending tended to add to the supply of its own funds.

Thus the growth of the market has contributed indirectly to world money expansion and price inflation. If the market had not come into existence, the chances are that the rate of price inflation in the later 1960s and 1970s would have been less. Correspondingly, the expansion of world trade and output may well have been more modest, although in the latter case the excesses which resulted in the weakening of the dollar, the oil price explosion and the halving of economic growth from 1973 would equally have been less pronounced.

The future role of the market and its consequences for the dollar

The Eurocurrency market is now crucial to the relatively smooth functioning of the world exchange system. The extent to which the market is now used both for recycling the payments surpluses of the oil-exporting countries and matching the deficits of other countries is far greater than the use of IMF facilities in assisting deficit countries. Moreover, the prospects of reform and expansion of the IMF system to the point where the dependence on the

[6]There is an extended version of this argument in CROCKETT, A.D. (1977). *International Money*. London; Nelson.

Eurocurrency market will begin to fade are remote. Banks, large businesses and national authorities, all make considerable use of this giant international capital market. It is the indirect vehicle of exchange rate adjustments, facilitating large currency transfers.

In the absence of an authoritative world system, as was initiated under the Bretton Woods Agreement, the Eurocurrency market will remain the principal feature of the world's monetary, exchange and reserve system. Indeed, the reserve role of the dollar is still enshrined within that system, for the greater part of the transactions within the market are designated in the US dollar. At the same time the market has facilitated the emergence of other currencies with a reserve role and to that extent the diversification of foreign currency reserves, even on a modest scale, has helped ease the US of part of the burden of having its currency used as the world's principal reserve asset.

It is also the case that the 1979–1980 round of oil price increases has resulted in even larger surpluses for the major oil-exporting countries and bigger deficits for the major importers. Thus the chances are that the Eurocurrency market will be the vehicle for recycling of funds on an even larger scale. Indeed, the consensus of forecasts is that the balance of supply and demand for oil through the 1980s will continue to be precarious, in spite of economies and the gradual development of new energy supplies. The general expectation is for world oil prices to continue to rise faster than the prices of manufactured products by around 4% per annum. For a number of years, therefore, it is probable that the payments imbalances associated with oil exports and imports will remain acute and that the role of the Eurocurrency market in facilitating the balancing transfers will remain crucial. There is no other working system in existence capable of meeting that need, nor any prospect of the nation states achieving the necessary compromises and agreements to institute an alternative system within the next few years.

This is not to say that the Eurocurrency system is without its faults and critics. Again, to quote the 1979 Annual Report of the BIS:

> It is difficult to deny that in the absence of the Euro-currency market dollar borrowings for the financing of hedging or speculative operations in the spot exchange markets would have been somewhat more difficult.

The facilities of the market have accentuated currency movements and swings in exchange rates from time to time to the embarrassment of domestic economies. Such pressures, however, assuming they arose from some fundamental disequilibrium, would ultimately have surfaced to force changes in any case. Even so, the scale of the Euromarket suggests it possesses a destabilizing potential when it is compared in size with domestic money supply. At the end of 1978, the funds deployed in the market were roughly twice the size of the US domestic money supply and relatively small movements of the Euromarket funds could proportionately be extremely powerful in relation to the domestic money supplies of countries such as Germany, the UK or Switzerland.

With these features in mind, and a belated recognition of the dangerous monetary expansion which may have been fuelled by inadequate attention to international banking operations, the central banks now seem likely to strengthen controls over their domestic banking systems with a view to exerting a stronger discipline over the Eurocurrency markets.

In an announcement following the April 1980 meeting of central bank governors of the BIS, it was stated that international bank lending aggregates had been expanding at 25% per annum, and that the contribution of the international banking system to recycling the large OPEC surpluses that have re-emerged, will lead to further substantial growth of these aggregates. The governors affirmed their agreement 'on the importance of maintaining the soundness and stability of the international banking system and of seeking to avoid any undesirable effects either worldwide or on the conduct of policy in particular countries.' The communiqué went on to say:

> With these conditions in mind, the governors have decided to strengthen regular and systematic monitoring of international banking developments, with a view to assessing their significance for the world economy, for the economies of individual countries, including particularly the operation of their domestic monetary policies, and for the soundness of the international banking system as a whole. A standing committee on Euromarkets will consider the international banking statistics compiled by the BIS and other relevant information and report to the governors at least twice a year, and more frequently if developments call for it. These arrangements for closer surveillance could provide a framework for intensifying, if appropriate, co-operation on monetary policies between the countries concerned.
>
> Recognizing that individual banks, or the international banking system as a whole, could in future be exposed to greater risks than in the past, the governors reaffirm the cardinal importance which they attach to the maintenance of sound banking standards—particularly with regard to capital adequacy, liquidity and concentration of risks. To this end, they place high priority on bringing into full effect the initiatives already taken by the Committee on Banking Regulations and Supervisory Practices, with regard to the supervision of banks' international business on a consolidated basis, improved assessment of country risk exposure, and the development of more comprehensive and consistent data for monitoring the extent of banks' maturity transformation.
>
> The governors note that differences in competitive conditions between domestic and international banking that arise out of official regulations and policies stimulate growth of international bank lending in general; and that transactions channelled through the Eurocurrency market can pose problems for the effectiveness of domestic monetary policy in those countries where such differences are particularly significant. The governors will continue efforts already being made to reduce the differences of competitive conditions, fully recognizing the difficulties arising from differences in the national structure and traditions of the banking system.

Although moving cautiously, the BIS has clearly recognized the problems and dangers inherent in the Eurocurrency market and the April 1980 communiqué suggests that central bank governors are aware of the need for tighter domestic monetary controls and disciplines. The concern over monetary inflation has increased to such an extent that the prospective growth of the international market seems certain to be far more modest than in the past.

Against that background we now examine the origins of the price inflation which has contributed to the decline of the Bretton Woods system and the emergence of a system of floating exchange rates.

5 Money, inflation and oil

Prices can only go up provided that money supply grows faster than the physical output of goods and services, or where the velocity of circulation is increased. As there is a practical physical limit to the rate of change in such velocity, it is broadly true to say that price inflation is brought about by 'too much money chasing too few goods'[1].

Under a gold standard system the volume of credit and money is directly determined by the amount of gold in the world's money system. Money supply increase is thus restricted to the extent of newly-mined gold entering the world's monetary reserves. In the absence of such a system, money expansion rests upon the expansion of the bank credit base engendered by government policies. For a stable money supply it is therefore necessary for fiscal and monetary policies to be fashioned in such a way as to prevent an expansion of the credit base, i.e. the level of bank deposits.

In the modern international scheme of things, given relatively free movement of capital and currency convertibility, monetary stability is only attainable where not one country but all conform to such a code of practice. That being said, it must be recognized that the self-interest of the banking community makes for a constant expansion of credit and money for bank profits are earned principally from bank advances. It is also in the interest of the banks to use money more efficiently, to mobilize idle funds and to stimulate the velocity of circulation. The electronics revolution aids that process and the development of large computer systems is speeding up money transfers not only within a country but between countries and thus contributes to an increase in the velocity of circulation. It may also be the case that velocity increases in this way without driving up interest rates, whereas without the technical facility to increase circulation a shortage of funds tends to drive up interest rates and induces an increase in velocity. Historically there is a close relationship between changes in velocity and interest rates and for purposes of interest rate analysis, this new technical feature of faster money transmission needs to be taken into account.

[1]To the best of my knowledge and belief, this simple definition was first given by Hugh Dalton when Chancellor of the Exchequer in the period 1946–1947.

A further feature making for increased velocity is the tendency for the population at large to use money more efficiently. Mistrust of banks, among other reasons, led many people in the past to 'tuck money under the mattress'. This practice appears to have declined and, if that is the case, velocity must have tended to increase for this reason.

If it is desirable, therefore, to aim for a general regime of a stable average price level, then money supply needs to be regulated so as to increase at a *slower* rate than the physical increase in output of goods and services. Thus if the long-run trend in output growth is 4% per annum, this being determined largely by the rate of ploughback out of income into productive investment, money growth needs to average less than 4% per annum to allow for a tendency for velocity of circulation to increase. For example:

	% per annum
Sustainable output growth	4
Average money growth	3
Contribution from velocity increase	1
Average rate of price inflation	nil

Yet the critical questions are: what is money?; how does it increase?; and what are the factors which generate money and price inflation?.

The history of prices

Historically, price inflation was at a modest average rate in Britain over many centuries until recent times. Price records for some commodities go back a long way. By linking these a continuous price history can be constructed back into the thirteenth century[2]. What stands out from such a history is the impact of the gold and silver influx into Europe in the sixteenth and seventeenth centuries and the periodic inflations directly associated with war, since wars are financed by increases in government borrowing (*Table 5.1*). It is also noteworthy that until the Second World War price inflation was generally reversed in the post-war periods.

A single episode also provides a vivid illustration of the link between money and prices. The Black Death reduced the population by at least one third. Yet there was no change in the amount of coin in circulation and just as much land available for cultivation as before. Labour was, therefore, extremely scarce in relation to the amount of money and the amount of land to be worked. Wages and prices rocketed and led to an official wage and price freeze imposed by Act of Parliament.

The major phases of inflation are shown in *Table 5.2*.

[2]PHELPS BROWN, E.H. and HOPKINS, SHEILA (November 1956). Seven Centuries of the Prices of Consumables compared with Builders' Wage Rates. *Economica*. London.

Table 5.1 History of the British National Debt 1688–1939 (£ million)

		Borrowed	*Repaid*	*Debt (at end of period)*
War	1688–1697	21	–	21
Peace	1697–1702	–	5	16
War	1702–1714	39	–	55
Peace	1714–1739	–	8	47
War	1739–1748	31	–	78
Peace	1748–1755	–	3	75
War	1755–1763	72	–	147
Peace	1763–1775	–	11	136
War	1775–1786	121	–	257
Peace	1786–1793	–	13	244
War	1793–1815	604	–	848
Peace	1815–1853	–	79	769
War	1853–1855	38	–	807
Peace	1855–1899	–	172	635
War	1899–1902	159	–	794
Peace	1902–1914	–	144	650
War	1914–1918	7180	–	7830
Peace	1918–1939	–	33*	7797*

Source: Bank of England
*There was a substantial amount of net debt repayment over the period which is concealed in the above figures, since they include the borrowing of the Exchange Equalization Fund and do not deduct the public debt held by public departments

Yet if money supply has tended to rise in such a way as to finance price inflation, we need to identify the pressures which result in such a money expansion. Up to the twentieth century price inflation could be attributed to the creation of excess money or the curtailment of supplies. Combinations of both these factors tend to prevail in wartime, thus bringing about more extreme price rises. Whether through clipping of coins and debasement of the currency or through the printing of money by governments and unregulated expansion of credit, money factors have always been of extreme importance so far as price inflation is concerned.

Table 5.2 The major phases of inflation

Period		*Average annual rate of increase in consumer prices (%)*
1268–1316	The First Debasement	2.4
1349–1352	Black Death	18.3
1509–1557	The Tudor Debasements	3.2
1789–1813	Napoleonic Wars	3.3
1913–1918	First World War	12.3
1938–1946	Second World War	6.6
1934–1968	Modern Inflation	4.3
1968–1980	The New Debasement	12.0
1268–1980		0.8

Sources: E.H. Phelps Brown and S. Hopkins: *Seven Centuries of the Price of Consumables. The British Economy, Key Statistics;* London Cambridge Economic Service. James Morrell and Associates' *Framework Forecasts.*

Inflation in the twentieth century

In the twentieth century we have witnessed a major change brought about by two new developments. The first has been the emergence of organized labour as a force first tending to stabilize wages and then to advance wages consistently through the years. This has altered the cost patterns of production and has helped even out the fluctuations in the business cycle. Whereas throughout the previous centuries the business cycle rose and fell with great severity, influenced to a large extent by fluctuations in climate and harvests, in the twentieth century manufacturing production has become of far greater importance. Costs and prices in manufacturing industry have tended to be 'administered' and not necessarily set in competitive open market conditions. It was also the case that wages could fall as well as rise in previous centuries and labour was regarded just as much a commodity in terms of costs of production as raw material. Without the protection of strong unions, employers were able to cut wages when trade slumped.

The second feature which marks out the twentieth century from its predecessors with regard to price inflation is the introduction of the concept of welfare in national politics and economics. Governments have been given a far greater role to play in national economies and they have been accorded responsibility for maintaining full employment and eliminating poverty. In one sense this has been due to the extension of the franchise. Democratic government based on 'one man, one vote' is a relatively recent phenomenon. The First World War marked a watershed in this respect with the overthrow of the European empires and their replacement by popular democracies. From the First World War onwards the power of the people has increased and politicians have quickly learned that they must respond to the pressures of popular opinion in order to win office and remain in power.

The dominant impact of the new democratic forces did not become fully apparent until after the Second World War. By then the position of governments as managers of their national economies had been fully established and the power of government, through control over vastly increased public spending, had reached a pinnacle of importance never achieved before.

These changes are reflected in the record of price movements throughout the twentieth century. In *Table 5.3* below the changes in consumer prices are shown for the US and the UK through various phases.

It will be seen that the changes in both countries in the years up to the First World War were modest but that prices were edging upwards. During the war years prices rose extremely rapidly and even though the US did not enter the war until some three years after the UK, US prices nevertheless showed large increases. In both countries prices declined in the 1920s. In the US the falls were more modest than in the UK where the excessive rises during the war appear to have been reversed more sharply.

In both countries prices fell in the slump with the US experiencing a more emphatic decline. Prices reached bottom in 1933 and, in the recovery, prices moved ahead again to a modest extent until the outbreak of the Second World War. From that time price inflation has been continuous. Neither country has experienced more than a single year in which the average price level has fallen. It is also of interest to note that from 1900 to 1948 the average annual rate of price increase for the two countries was not markedly different. But from 1948

Table 5.3 US and UK consumer price changes from 1900

Period	*Average annual rate of change*	
	US (%)	*UK* (%)
1900–1914	2.1	1.1
1914–1920	8.3	16.8
1920–1929	–0.7	–3.7
1929–1933	–7.7	–2.9
1933–1939	1.6	1.5
1939–1948	6.9	6.7
1948–1952	2.3	5.0
1952–1968	1.6	2.9
1968–1980	7.6	12.0
1900–1948	2.3	2.7
1948–1980	3.9	6.7

Source: *The British Economy, Key Statistics.* IMF Financial Statistics

onwards the UK rate of price inflation has been well in excess of the US average.

The New Deal and the welfare state

As we have seen, the turning point in respect of price inflation came with the recovery from the slump of the 1930s. As production began to expand so prices edged forward. Even so, the rate of price increase, in both the US and the UK, averaged no more than 1½% per annum in the six years from 1933 to 1939. In the case of the US this was a smaller rate of price increase than in the period preceding the First World War. The real turning point, therefore, appears to have come rather later. If the war period is discounted, and the pace of price inflation was very much lower in the Second World War than in the First World War, then the watershed, so far as inflation is concerned, must have been in the post-war period. Indeed, in the US the rate of inflation continued to be extremely modest by today's standards up until the second half of the 1960s.

The nature of price movements has been completely different from 1933 onwards. Throughout the course of the subsequent 47 years, prices have been less erratic than at any time in previous history. The direction has been consistently upwards. The key lies in the political developments following the deep depression of the early 1930s. Unemployment reached unprecedented levels. At the worst point more than three million people were registered as unemployed in the UK and before Hitler came to power in Germany unemployment had reached the horrific level of eight millions. Conditions were equally bad in the US where the collapse of thousands of banks led to multiple business failures and a huge drop in spending and production.

Confronted with economic crisis on this scale few governments had the vision or courage to realize that they alone could restore confidence through expanding public sector spending, first to offset the cutbacks of a demoralized general public, and then to generate a rise in total spending and output of the economy at large. Faced with financial failures and balance of payments problems, governments fell into the error of adopting policies of retrenchment and balanced budgets, thereby exacerbating the general problem. At the same time, however, there was a growing awareness and understanding of the problem of inadequate purchasing power and its contribution to unemployment.

The lesson of the Second World War was quite emphatic in this respect, and it became abundantly clear that large scale increases in public sector spending, which were not compensated by matching increases in tax revenues, had been the means of stimulating output and overcoming unemployment. Thus, the experiments in the 1930s with the New Deal policies and the experiences of the economic impact of the Second World War, taught politicians the way in which unemployment could be cured. Large public sector deficit spending and easy fiscal policy became the tools of meeting the democratic demands for full employment. At the same time the concept of welfare was introduced into political programmes. Dole queues and soup kitchens generated widescale interest in schemes for social security and national insurance. The idea of a safety net for the whole of society to ensure that no one need be faced with the prospect of dire poverty and starvation became the order of the day. Existing schemes were improved and during the war years programmes were established to be brought into operation in the post-war reconstruction period.

These are the features which have led to conditions in which the character of price movements has altered, and price falls through the economy at large are now virtually impossible. At the same time the degree of price fluctuation from year to year has been reduced while the pattern of changes has now brought about a continuous rise in the price level.

Cost pressures

In the final analysis virtually all costs can be attributed to labour. Apart from its direct labour bill, a firm, when buying materials and components, energy and services, is buying other people's labour in an indirect way. Thus, even imports can be thought of as a labour cost—in this case the labour of foreign workers. In broad terms then, cost pressures can be measured by taking the change in home labour costs with the change in import prices.

The major change in the economic environment affecting costs has been the advent of the industrial trade union. It was not until the end of the nineteenth century that the unions became a major force in pushing up wage levels. During the century the working population rose extremely rapidly. In the twentieth century the population has grown far more slowly than during the nineteenth century. Skilled labour has become relatively scarce. Therefore its bargaining position has been enhanced considerably.

Moreover the power of the trade union has not diminished; if anything its influence over wages has increased. In an age where technological advance is rapid, the demand for labour skills continues to rise. Skilled labour is always in short supply and the chances are that in future years the wage level will be increasingly dictated by demand for skill. In the face of this it would be unwise to postulate anything other than a continued rise in the level of wage earnings.

If, as a consequence, wage costs per unit of output rise, prices too must also be expected to rise. Since 1968, when the May disturbances in Paris led to sharp and inflationary wage increases, the western economies have been plagued with persistently high wage settlements. These have been arrived at in some years in the face of conditions of credit shortage, dear money and rising unemployment, thus refuting the traditional economic analysis. At the same time, there has been an increasing tendency towards social unrest and violence.

For these reasons it is appropriate to question the use of historical economic cyclical relationships. Social pressures have a new impact, not only on economic performance, but on national economic management. The question, therefore, must be faced whether the basic trends are changing more rapidly and, if so, what will be the reactions of society at large and their elected governments.

At the national scale it still takes several years for major changes in policies of economic management to evolve. Immediately after the Second World War, governments were concerned both with reconstruction and the need to avoid the mass unemployment which characterized the inter-war period. In the 1950s these policies were moderated and a major change took place throughout the western world. Regulation of national economies through monetary discipline became the order of the day. 'Market', or laissez-faire, policies were pursued and interest rates were allowed to rise. Dear money policies characterized the 1960s culminating in a worldwide interest rate peak in 1974, and then a new peak in 1980.

The new money explosion

Although the social pressures stimulating consumer demand and the drive for higher and higher incomes contribute to price inflation, it is still the case that money itself is a prerequisite for price rises. Yet price increases since the Second World War can be largely explained from the cost side by the analysis of labour costs per unit of output. The sharp acceleration in both wage and price increases has therefore led to speculation as to its causes. It is suggested, for example, that new pressures are at work and that the social factors have led to surges in wage demands. A variety of reasons is given such as frustration due to controls holding down the standard of living. The pressures of advertising, too, constantly whet consumer appetites. There is also the question of expectations. A high level of price increases in one year will generate a high level of wage demands in the following year. Thus high prices generate continuing expectations of further high price rises.

It will be apparent, however, that inflation cannot occur on this scale unless employers are both willing and able to grant high wage increases. If wage demands are particularly high, but employers are unable to meet them because of the sharp erosion of profits by cost increases, these demands will inevitably be resisted more forcefully. The question arises, therefore, how is it that employers have been able to grant excessive wage increases?

As we have observed, price inflation through the ages amounts in the last resort to too much money chasing too few goods. In other words, in virtually all cases the explanation lies in the excess of money. However, there are powerful social and political pressures which militate against governments pursuing consistent tight money policies and it remains broadly true to say no national scheme to curb inflation can be expected to succeed unless ways are found of holding wage increases in check.

For an open economy, dependent upon foreign trade both for supplies of imports and export markets, the rate of wage inflation in other countries will determine, in part, the domestic rate of inflation. With this factor to be taken into account is also follows that no country, unless it is almost entirely self-sufficient, will be able to cure the inflationary problem in isolation. All the trading nations must simultaneously adopt and persist with counter-inflation policies with particular emphasis on wage limitation to back up money curbs, if inflation is to be gradually brought under control.

Inflation generated by wage increases is still dependent upon a supply of money in sufficient quantity to facilitate both higher wages and prices. To lay the blame for accelerating inflation solely at the door of labour would be a gross injustice. The worldwide wage and price explosion dating from 1968 undoubtedly had its origins in the expansionary policies of US fiscal policy. In attempting to overcome a minor recession and to continue the financing of the Vietnam War, US spending and production were vigorously re-expanded. The secondary effects of this on other countries were pronounced.

In all the analysis of the causes of the modern inflation the search for relationships has not been particularly fruitful. One major omission has been to discuss how wage bargains are struck with employers and trade union negotiators. In this connection it will frequently be found that employers are concerned, not only to retain labour, but to protect their employees and at least to maintain their living standards. This entails a piece of simple arithmetic in which the increase in the Retail Price Index is translated into a matching increase in after-tax pay.

Many employers approach the problem of pay increases in this way. Where the pressures on costs are greater than the market will bear in terms of higher prices, then the employer is forced to find ways of economizing in the use of labour and natural wastage will be allowed to take place to reduce the numbers employed and to offset in part the rise in the labour bill. Similarly, union negotiators will have this same requirement in mind and where it seems likely that prices will rise faster than in the past, the wage requirement will be pitched higher still. It may be, therefore, that wage demands are determined both by price increases since the last settlement as well as by expected rates of inflation.

Another factor to be taken into the reckoning on the social side is that none of us likes to be below the average. Where the figures for wage levels are well publicized (and the professional negotiators are well aware of increases achieved by other unions) it then becomes extremely difficult for the negotiators to accept increases which compare unfavourably with those achieved in other industries. The fact that a below-average situation is unacceptable means that there is a constant tendency to attempt to catch up or leap ahead. This would appear to be one of the outcomes of free wage bargaining.

There thus appears to be a natural tendency in an unfettered market for wages and prices to accelerate. Any forecasts of inflation should take this normal sequence into account, as well as the fact that we live in a highly materialist society where consumer appetites appear to be constantly expanding.

This is not to say, however, that wages are the cause of inflation. Rather, the situation is quite clearly that social pressures under a free system will make for rising inflation. The key to this pattern of behaviour lies in the weakness of the democratic system. So long as politicians are frightened of taking action to break the spiral and to impose unpopular remedies, the tendency will be for governments to adopt monetary and fiscal policies which are passive and thus accommodate the mounting inflation.

The importance of social pressures

The stimulus to consumer appetites has made an impact not only on the demand for wages but has been manifested in other important ways. In the first place family income is supplemented by full-time or part-time work by the housewife. Born initially of necessity, the wife and mother now chooses to go out to work both to create and supplement discretionary spending power to pay for holidays, a better home and so on, as well as to escape from the home and its drudgery. With the housewife out at work it becomes still more necessary to adopt labour saving techniques in the home, thus helping to eliminate drudgery. This includes the installation of a wide range of electrical appliances and the consumption of labour saving products such as convenience foods. These are factors tending to spur on demands for higher incomes.

Beyond doubt, women have now attained a greater degree of personal freedom and the signs are that emancipation will be pursued just as vigorously in the next decade. It is no coincidence that the birthrate continues to fall.

Another effect of the stimulation of consumer appetites can be found in work patterns. In the US the reduction of the working week has made it increasingly possible for men to take second, part-time jobs. 'Moonlighting' is now widespread in the US and throughout Europe and, as average working hours are reduced, there will undoubtedly be an increase in moonlighting.

A further implication of the social pressures bearing on work and working hours is the growing resistance to abnormal working time. Night shifts are becoming more difficult to man. Families tend to want common leisure hours and common holidays. This being so, production may have to be concentrated in fewer working hours with a high proportion of idle plant time. In turn, this will create a need for higher capacity machinery and a reorganization of plants to facilitate much higher labour output per man hour. This is another reason for looking for a faster rate of growth in labour saving investment.

Concern with health is also a social factor of growing importance. Man, by nature, will always be concerned with his fitness and well-being. This is reflected in literature down the ages. In modern times, however, the stresses and strains have changed. The fear of illness has lessened as medical knowledge and skills have advanced. But the stresses through changes in work, diet and family circumstances have probably become greater. The economic significance of concern for health is that demand is virtually limitless for processes which may prolong life and maintain activity. Medical knowledge is advancing steadily in these directions and there is likely to be a strong growth in demand for health services. Since there is already an abnormally high proportion of old people in the population, it will be seen that the extension of the provision of health service through the state may well become a political issue of growing importance. This, too, has inflationary consequences.

Educational patterns also have great significance in determining the way of life and have consequences for inflation. The number of graduates and qualified people in the population has risen rapidly. Regardless of the kind of jobs these people obtain—and they will not all find positions of responsibility—the pattern of life and spending of their families will be influenced more by their educational backgrounds than their jobs. In other words, demands are not likely to be matched by productivity from this section of the community.

An unpleasant social factor which must not be disregarded is the trend towards increasing violence and crime. Life has always been violent and only on rare occasions has society at large been comparatively law abiding. The frustrations due to boring jobs and lack of educational attainment have increased. Television has helped to promulgate violence. In addition, violent protest appears to be rewarded, attracting public attention to a cause, whereas normal negotiations and representations sometimes appear to fail to produce results. The democratic processes are slow and long-winded and we therefore postulate a continued rise in violent protest and militancy. This, too, will be reflected in wage inflation.

The importance of politics

Inflation is therefore unlikely to be eliminated. On balance the forces making for the continuation of inflation are particularly powerful, and wage increases are not the only reason why it can be postulated that inflation will continue. For one thing, full employment is accepted policy throughout the advanced world. When it comes to economic issues electorates generally have short memories. The most important influences at times of elections appear to be the immediate level of money wages, the degree of unemployment and the level of prices in the shops. Since politicians have a natural tendency to cling to power and elections of one kind or another occur at fairly frequent intervals, the pressures of modern democracy tend to make for continuous full employment policies. This is a worldwide tendency, so that inflation in one country tends to influence the level of prices in others, and no government would expect to be re-elected on a policy of full-blooded retrenchment and deflation.

Neither would such a policy be practicable in this day and age, for the growth in government welfare spending is also inevitable. Social burdens are increasing steadily. Not only are young people staying for longer periods at school and university, but the tendency is for old people to be kept alive longer. The dependent population will ultimately grow faster than the population at work. The burden of maintaining non-productive elements of the community is borne through taxation. Thus governments cannot escape the need to finance education on the one hand and health and retirement on the other. Moreover, the tendencies in medicine are to facilitate prolongation of life by extremely costly methods.

It follows, therefore, that the scope for tax reduction is limited, and because of the dislike of high taxation, there will always be a temptation for the politician to resort to deficit financing. Wherever practicable, governments will wish to continue to borrow from the general public and the banks. For this reason governments run the risk of increasing money supply in an inflationary way.

In private and commercial life there has been a strong increase in the use of credit. When the levels of personal debt are compared between the US and Europe, it will be seen that there is a long gap between the use of credit in the two regions. The trend in the use of credit is steadily upwards. In addition, as we have noted, there is an increasing efficiency in the use of money. Both these tendencies, namely the more efficient use of money and the greater use of credit, will tend to foster a rise in prices, and the social pressures will push politicians towards adopting accommodating credit and monetary policies.

It appears, therefore, that democratic and social pressures tend to thwart attempts to control and eliminate inflation. It may even be that the system contains the seeds of its own destruction. The various measures which are necessary to combat inflation are precisely those which will prove most unpopular in political terms and are least likely to be sustained by governments for any length of time. Severe deflationary policies are either unlikely to be initiated in the first place or to be continued for a sufficient length of time to restore a non-inflationary position. At the same time controls which inhibit individual freedom to optimize personal income are unlikely to be maintained effectively because of their widespread unpopularity both with employees and with businessmen subject to price restraints.

On balance, therefore, it would be naive to suggest that inflation is going to subside in the western democracies without a painful adjustment. Indeed, it is necessary to ask whether the democratic systems will in fact survive. Should the inflationary pressures worsen and accelerating inflation lead to lower living standards and severe social disruption, then the democratic regimes may be doomed to be replaced by authoritarian systems of the Right or Left. It remains to be seen whether or not politicians will emerge from the pack with the foresight and courage to explain to the people at large the nature of the inflationary problems and the sacrifices needed to restore stable conditions, so as to facilitate steady growth in output and the standard of living.

Oil

All these arguments suggest that price inflation will continue even without taking into account the world energy crisis.

The world energy crisis is real. Left to market forces, the oil shortage would force all energy prices to a sufficient level to stifle demand. The high prices of energy would stimulate the search for new energy sources and would increase potential reserves. Thus it is argued there is no potential energy problem.

The reality is, however, that energy production is not left to unfettered market forces and is subject to political intervention and control. It is also the case that the price levels established as a result of high and rising levels of demand, produce hardships for a large proportion of the world's population. The sacrifices required to secure even lower amounts of energy consumption imply distortions in other patterns of production and consumption which are tantamount to crisis conditions for many countries. The nature of the problem is well illustrated in *Table 5.4*, showing the marked contrasts in energy consumption per head for different countries.

Energy consumption in the US is more than five times the world average. Energy consumption in China and India, countries accounting for a third of the

Table 5.4 Energy consumption per head

	Selected countries: 1978 (tonnes oil equivalent)
USA	8.8
Western Europe	3.0
Japan	3.1
Rest of the World	0.9
World average	1.6

Source: BP Statistical Review of the World Oil Industry, 1978

world's population, is at only one-fifth of the world average. Quite clearly the potential growth in demand for energy from the less developed areas of the world is vast, and even if the growth in energy consumption were to be halted in the advanced countries, rising living standards elsewhere would force up the growth in world energy consumption in such a way as to perpetuate the oil shortage.

Up to the crisis of 1973 world energy consumption grew in line with total world output (GNP). In round figures output and energy consumption expanded at an average rate close to 5% per annum. The pattern of energy consumption is shown in *Table 5.5*, the dominant position of coal rapidly giving way to oil.

Table 5.5 World energy consumption by source

	1925 (%)	*1950* (%)	*1972* (%)	*1978* (%)
Coal	83	61	33	27
Oil	13	28	46	46
Natural gas	3	10	18	19
Hydro, nuclear and other	1	1	3	8
Total	100	100	100	100

Source: BP Statistical Review of the World Oil Industry; various years

Since the quadrupling of oil prices in 1973–1974, oil has maintained its share of supplies, in spite of the recession and the motives to economize on oil consumption. Gas and nuclear energy have increased their contribution while coal's share has continued to decline.

The dependence on oil has become excessive and through the 1970s the world has been consuming oil products faster than new supplies are being discovered. Annual consumption in the non-communist world now exceeds new discoveries by some three billion barrels per year.

Even with the more sophisticated methods of search and recovery, proven oil reserves are unlikely to keep pace with present levels of consumption. It is therefore inescapable that the rate of oil consumption has to be reduced and other forms of energy have to replace oil. The transition will be lengthy and painful.

Future world energy demand

The ratio of energy consumption to output growth has already dropped from its previous 1:1 ratio, and for forecasting purposes it must be assumed that a lower ratio will be maintained. It has taken a second crisis in 1979 to reinforce the message that the world's potential appetite for oil cannot be satisfied in the short-run and can only be met in the longer-run given fundamental changes in energy consumption and energy production through newer technologies. Until that has been achieved, the world will need to economize in the use of oil. Throughout the 1980s, therefore, high energy prices will strengthen the incentives to economize and a gradual rise seems likely in the efficiency of energy production and consumption. This is illustrated in *Table 5.6*.

Table 5.6 Energy consumption in the 1980s

World output growth	2½–4% per annum
Energy co-efficient	0.7:1–0.9:1
Energy consumption	2–3% per annum

Lower output growth would lessen the pressures to economize in energy consumption and, conversely, faster output growth would strengthen the economy effects. We therefore forecast growth in world energy consumption at between 2 and 3% per annum through the decade.

So far as potential supplies are concerned, world coal reserves are estimated at three hundred years at present rates of consumption. Russia, the US and China possess over 90% of potential reserve and in the long-run coal could satisfy a large part of the world's potential energy requirements. However, the problem with coal in the short-run is its inflexibility which therefore limits its energy application. Apart from being a dirty and high polluting fuel, in the majority of cases it is mined underground in difficult and costly conditions and, with the long investment time required to develop new mines, the contribution of coal to world energy requirements can only be expanded at a slow pace. Proven gas reserves, on the other hand, are estimated to have a life of only fifty years at current rates of consumption. The prospect is that gas supplies will only increase slowly through the next decade and at a slower rate than energy consumption as a whole.

Nuclear power, however, is capable of almost indefinite expansion. The limiting factors are, first, the rate of investment in nuclear power stations and secondly, the political concern over the possible dangers from radiation through accidents in the productive process. The anti-nuclear lobby appears to be gaining strength and restrictions have been imposed on the development of nuclear energy in a number of countries. At least 22 countries have installed electricity-producing reactors so far. Both the UK and the US have been generating between 13% and 14% of national electricity supplies from nuclear reactors and this fraction is likely to increase to 20% by the mid-1980s. However, the accident at the atomic plant on Three Mile Island in 1979 seems likely to slow down the pace of nuclear development and nuclear power is unlikely to expand fast enough to reduce dependence on oil through the 1980s.

Other sources of energy, apart from oil, such as hydro-electric power and solar energy, contribute less than 8% to world energy supplies. Since the technology for gathering solar energy is in its infancy and is extremely costly, little can be expected from solar energy supplies in the 1980s. Wind and wave power are also in their infancy so far as prospective mass supplies of energy are concerned, and these miscellaneous potential sources of energy supply will not be major contributors to world energy needs within the next decade.

Inevitably, therefore, oil remains the balancing item in the world energy equation. Until new sources of energy are available in greater abundance the dependence on oil remains. This is illustrated in *Table 5.7* for the non-communist world.

Table 5.7 Energy balance (Non-communist world)

	1976	*1990*	*Increase*
	(billions of tonnes of oil equivalent)		(% per annum)
Total energy	4.6	7.4	2.8
contributed by			
Coal	0.9	1.5	0.6
Gas	0.8	1.1	0.3
Nuclear	0.1	0.6	0.5
Hydro-, etc.	0.3	0.6	0.3
Oil to balance	2.5	3.6	1.1

Source: World Energy Prospects, Dr A.W. Pearce, *ESSO Magazine*, No. 110 Spring 1979

The estimates imply growth rates of 3% per annum for total energy demand and 2½% per annum for oil. These figures are at the top end of our forecast range but take no account of the position in the communist world. It is not generally recognized that in spite of its huge energy reserves the USSR may well turn from being an oil exporter to an oil importer in the 1980s[3]. Although currently the world's largest oil producer, at a rate of 11 million barrels a day compared with 8½ million for Saudi Arabia, oil demand in the USSR and her

Table 5.8 Oil supply and demand (Non-communist countries)

	1976	*1990*
	(billions of tonnes)	
Total demand	2.5	3.6
Total supply	2.5	3.6
Made up from:		
Imports available	0.1	0.1
US and Canada	0.6	0.5
Europe	0.1	0.3
Other Non-OPEC	0.2	0.5
OPEC—Outside Mid-East	0.4	0.5
OPEC—Middle East	1.1	1.7

Source: World Energy Prospects, Dr A.W. Pearce, *ESSO Magazine*, No. 110 Spring 1979

[3]However, a recent study asserts that the USSR's oil-producing potential has been substantially understated in the West: *Soviet Proved Oil Reserves, 1946–1980*. Petrostudies; Malmo, Sweden.

client countries is likely to outstrip supplies within the next few years. There is thus a strong motive in the communist countries, too, to economize in oil consumption and to develop alternative sources of energy in order to avoid dependence on western supplies of oil.

Thus the dependence on the OPEC suppliers seems certain to continue throughout the 1980s. As *Table 5.8* indicates the western world will still be dependent for nearly half of its oil supplies on the Middle East by 1990, and if anything that dependence will have increased.

The price of oil

Oil prices will continue to be fixed by political decision, rather than by traders in the open market. The leading oil producers have shown growing concern about the ultimate depletion of reserves and are pursuing cautious policies with regard to production levels.

Although Saudi Arabia, for example, could lift production levels above the current rate of around 8½ million barrels per day, she is unlikely to do so other than to meet temporary world problems such as arose in 1979 through the disruption of Iranian production. Other countries, too, notably Venezuela, Kuwait and Iran are restricting output levels, so that prospects for the expansion of world oil production through the 1980s must be modest. Mexican production will begin to make a significant contribution to world supplies later in the decade, but it seems unlikely that world production levels will rise by more than about 2% per annum from just over 60 million barrels a day to 75 million by 1990. This also assumes that China will become a major producer but that she is likely to consume the greater part of her own output.

A rate of growth of 2% per annum would be consistent with the lower end of our forecast range for energy consumption growth. To limit consumption in this way means that oil consumers will need to restrict demand through high and rising prices. Whereas this seems likely in the majority of countries and will tend to stabilize oil consumption in many cases, the US and some faster growing countries are still likely to increase their levels of oil consumption. President Carter's energy programme seems unlikely to produce significant results until later in the century. While oil prices in the US are so far below those ruling in other countries, the pressures to economize remain small. As we have seen US energy consumption is vast by comparison with the world average and, because of the growth in the young adult population resulting from the baby boom of the late 1950s and early 1960s, the number of households will go on rising through the next few years, bringing about an inevitable increase in the US car park. The total number of vehicles in use still seems likely to rise from around 140 million today to some 160 million in 1985, a rate of growth of more than 2½% per annum[4].

The gradual shift to smaller car size and the gradual introduction of electronic controls of petrol injection in vehicles will contribute to oil economy in the 1980s. Also during the decade we foresee substantial technical progress in the development of a hydrogen-based internal combustion engine. Its

[4]DOWNS, ANTHONY (July 1979). Population Explosion—of Automobiles. *Across the Board*. New York

contribution to oil economy will be negligible, however, in the 1980s, although in the 1990s we believe aircraft are likely to be fuelled by hydrogen as will motor vehicles to an increasing extent.

Experience during the 1970s, since the quadrupling of the price of oil, shows some economy in oil consumption associated with the resultant recession. In the subsequent recovery oil consumption expanded again. Throughout the period oil prices were raised but generally by less than the increase in average prices of manufactured goods in the OECD countries. The 1979 oil price rises restored the position to the equivalent price peak of 1974, but the increases in 1980 have pushed relative prices above that base point. In other words, with a relatively modest increase in the real price of oil over the five year period, oil consumption has still gone on rising.

With the greater concern to economize in levels of oil production, the restricted levels of output which we foresee seem likely to bring about above-average price rises for oil in order to restrict consumption growth. We therefore put extremely low odds on the price of oil remaining stable in relation to other prices, and we assume there is a high probability of oil prices rising in real terms by an average of something like 4% per annum.

The price profile is likely to be erratic, with economies in consumption and the effects of the short-term recession checking oil price increases in the first years of the decade. Assuming a cyclical upturn in world industrial production from 1981–1982, then rising demand for oil seems likely to push up prices again (and perhaps sharply) in the period between 1982 and 1984.

Oil price rises on this scale inevitably push up costs. Since oil prices have become a benchmark for other prices, all energy costs are likely to increase at an above-average rate; and since energy accounts for around 10% of all costs, the price rises envisaged will continue to generate an unwelcome degree of cost inflation.

Whether or not this has a general effect on price inflation depends critically upon the rate of money supply increase and the rise of purchasing power in current prices. If overall purchasing power is restricted, the extra money needed to buy energy will lead to less money and purchasing power for other things and would thus perpetuate the depression of output as a whole. This would be consistent with a counter-inflation programme of reduced government deficits and declining growth in money supply.

The important question will therefore be political; can democratically elected governments resist the pressures for measures to stimulate spending and output aimed at creating more jobs? Since counter-inflation policies are deflationary, as is the rise in energy costs, unemployment will tend to be forced up. This, coupled with the natural increase in the size of the potential labour force in all countries in the 1980s, will give rise to powerful social and political pressures to mitigate the rise in unemployment. Indeed, technical change and the determination of employers to curb labour costs and to reduce numbers employed will add to those pressures.

The inevitability of price inflation

We have outlined the social pressures making for a continued inflationary pressure on governments and wages. But there are other factors of varying degrees of importance tending to add to this inflationary pressure. An additional factor leading to a general rise in the price level is the inability of the service-producing sector to absorb rising costs. The major gains in labour productivity are achieved by the manufacturing industries. In some cases the rise in productivity is sufficiently large to offset the rise in costs. Nevertheless, we seldom find that manufacturing products are reduced in price. In other words, the chance of the community benefiting through price reductions is small.

In a number of service industries it is extremely difficult to avoid price increases. Since wages tend to rise in line throughout the economy, service industries are compelled to pay rising wages. However, in many instances the opportunities for increasing labour productivity in service activities are extremely limited. In the professions such as teaching, productivity is difficult to measure in any case. The chances are that output per man in this kind of field is virtually static. The same must be true of services such as hairdressing or plumbing. The rate of increase in labour productivity is undeniably small. Therefore, in order to facilitate a rising standard of living for workers in service fields, prices have to go up. Unless price rises in the service sector can be offset by price cuts from the manufacturing sectors, inflation will be inevitable. So far there is no evidence from any country to suggest that a combination of price reductions and price increases between the sectors has been achieved in such a way as to produce overall price stability.

Another factor making for inflation is the scarcity of land. Since land is a fixed item of production, in the sense that the quantity of land cannot be meaningfully increased, land will continue to have a growing scarcity value in relation to the world's population. It is inevitable that land prices will continue to rise and, in so far as land features as a cost of production, it will impart an element of cost inflation. Rents are determined to a certain extent by land prices and since rent, or its equivalent in terms of house ownership, is an important factor in the cost of living, it will be seen that land scarcity and rising land values will be another long-term inflationary factor.

The realization of this situation is probably an additional element contributing to the maintenance of inflation. The awareness of the attractions of holding real as opposed to monetary assets has spread to most parts of the community. Just as land is seen to have a scarcity value, other fixed assets are believed to hold attractions by virtue of their ability to protect the owner against inflation. We have been witnessing in recent years a movement out of money into real assets and the acceptance of the inevitability of inflation, which such a movement implies, makes it extremely difficult to reverse this tendency. In other words, the acceptance of inflation is likely to ensure its continuation for a number of years yet.

We may therefore summarize the various long-term pressures making for the continuance of inflation in some degree, as follows:

(1) Skilled labour will be scarce
(2) The power of organized labour will remain strong
(3) Money wages will continue to rise faster than labour productivity
(4) There are worldwide political pressures for full employment
(5) Welfare spending on education, the aged and health will require growing amounts of government spending, and will also exert increasing pressure on the working population through increased social security taxation
(6) There is every expectation of an expansion in the use of credit

(7) Service industries are generally unable to absorb rising costs, and since services account for a growing share of output, the prospects of offsetting price rises in this area are slim
(8) The scarcity of land will lead to rising land prices and higher rents
(9) The general realization of the fact of inflation has produced a preference for eal assets rather than money
(10) War in some form or other is a permanent feature of the world scene. In consequence, inflationary forces will always be at work in some part of the globe as a result of war, tending to force up prices of exports and imports. Large trading countries will tend to import an element of inflation
(11) Energy costs will continue to rise
(12) Governments have a natural tendency to prefer deficit financing to rising taxation. This implies that the money supply will tend to be increased too fast, with inflationary consequences.

The future rate of inflation

It can, however, still be argued that inflation should not be considered inevitable if only because the management of the economy can be expected to become more expert. An important feature of modern life is the steady advance in all brances of knowledge. The authorities now know how to manage demand within certain limits. The workings of the credit and monetary system on the one hand and the impact of changes in government spending and taxation on the other, are probably sufficiently well understood to lead to the adoption of policies offering some degree of success in reducing price inflation. Yet the institutional mechanism required for the stabilization of wages and prices will need to be established in all countries before inflation can be eradicated. If not, inflation will be imported through a general raising of the prices of goods and services in international trade.

For these reasons it is unrealistic to anticipate that the leading industrial nations will succeed in developing economic management in such a way as to prevent price inflation for at least another 20 years.

The major changes required to achieve a stable price level are:

(1) International harmonization of domestic economic policies
(2) Careful control of fiscal policies so as to prevent government borrowing expanding in such a way as to drive up the money supply
(3) Strong control over the banks and the expansion of credit
(4) International control over movements of funds so as to prevent rapid credit expansion through international capital markets such as the Eurodollar system
(5) The adoption of policies, preferably by voluntary agreement, to halt the abuse of the monopoly power of labour

Will the new price inflation be curbed or will the tempo continue to accelerate, bringing ruin in its train? The changes in economic management required to achieve stability are too great to be implemented quickly. Effective international agreements are notoriously difficult to achieve and it would be unrealistic to expect the present excesses to be cured in less than a decade. In the interval, if matters go from bad to worse, there appear to be four alternative outcomes. First, dissatisfaction with the ability of a democratically elected government to maintain economic order could lead to a form of anarchy leading in turn to authoritarian rule. Right wing dictatorship, mandated to restore order and to implement tough (anti-labour) policies is a distinct possibility. Secondly, the inability of business to function adequately under extreme price inflation and hampered by controls, may lead to extensive socialization and ultimately to severe left wing authoritarian government. Thirdly, the tempo of price inflation may 'frighten' governments into 'realistic' policies.

Finally, there may be a gradual movement towards indexation, because western governments are incapable of adopting radical solutions in a hurry, giving us the worst of both worlds. High rates of inflation would persist, along with its injustices, and the difficulties of doing business would lead to a protracted recession. This last course seems likely unless governments move sensibly and quickly.

Some degree of price inflation appears to be inevitable. For a long period ahead it must be assumed that the *minimum* rate of average price increase will be 2% per annum. That rate must, for practical purposes, be regarded as virtual price stability. In the short-run, the peak of world inflation in 1980 was lower than in the previous peak in 1974–1975 and current policies suggest a gradual decline in the rate of price inflation in the 1980s. Although this seems the most probable outcome so far as inflation is concerned, it must be conceded that if governments fail to make the necessary adjustments through monetary correction, then the social pressures outlined above could explode, producing severe setbacks in terms of output and trade.

Against that background we examine in the following chapter the prospects for price inflation and the consequences for the US dollar.

6

Future inflation and its impact on the dollar

The decline in the dollar from the early 1970s originated in the persistent US payments deficits and the gradual erosion of foreign confidence in the dollar as a store of value. The accumulation of dollars outside the US had reached a point where other countries were unwilling to go on adding to their holdings of liquid dollar balances.

One of the underlying reasons for the crisis of the 1970s was the increase in price inflation in the US. The value of foreign holdings of the dollar was being gradually eroded in real terms. The problem was exacerbated by the quadrupling of oil prices in 1973–1974 in two ways. First, US oil imports soared in value, deepening the balance of payments deficit and increasing the dollar outflows and the dollar balances held by the oil exporting countries. Secondly, the rise in oil prices forced up costs and exacerbated the inflationary pressures. Since the US money supply was also rising at an excessive rate, price inflation increased sharply, as was also the case with the other major industrial oil-importing countries.

The effect was to deepen the dollar crisis and the problems of surplus dollars in the world economy. The sequence was repeated with the doubling of oil prices in 1979–1980, the cost inflation again being fuelled with an excessive rate of increase in the US money supply. Measures were then taken to reduce the rate of money growth and various controls were introduced aimed at curbing the growth of bank credit. By this time the value of the dollar in relation to the world's major currencies had declined to the point where the dollar was undervalued on a purchasing power comparison by around 20%.

For the dollar to regain its acceptability as a world reserve asset and as a unit in general use in world commerce, it is clearly necessary to restore confidence in the dollar as a store of value. In other words, holders of dollars have to be convinced that its purchasing power will not be eroded by price inflation, at least by comparison with alternative currency investment outlets. For this to happen, the US rate of price inflation has to be brought down to the average of other leading countries, notably Germany and Japan, and then brought down further to an acceptable long-term level. If, for example, the inflation rate were to be brought down to an average of 1.6% per annum, which had been the case for the period from 1952 to 1968, there would be a sufficient restoration of confidence in the dollar for the problem of the world reserve system to be solved and for the acceptance of a dollar standard.

What, then, is the prospect for price inflation in the US in the future?

Inflationary pressures

As was observed in the previous chapter, there are varied factors making for persistent price inflation. Apart from the difficulties of holding money growth down to a point where it does not finance future price increases, there are powerful social and political forces tending to create inflationary pressures. Since labour unions exist both to promote their members' interests and to protect them, there is a tendency for wages to be forced up at least to compensate for current rates of price inflation. To raise the purchasing power and standard of living of workers, pay rises have to exceed the going rate of price inflation.

Moreover, with relatively high unemployment and a natural increase in the size of the potential labour force resulting from the high birthrates of the late 1950s and early 1960s, governments are under considerable pressure to expand spending power and demand so as to create more jobs. The tendency, therefore, in a political democracy such as the US, is for the government of the day to pursue expansionary budgets. This results in an excess of government spending over revenues and the resultant financial deficits have to be financed by a high level of borrowing. If the scale of the borrowing is large enough in relation to private savings, the tendency will be for government borrowing to have an expansionary effect on the money supply. With frequent elections and the natural desire for governments at federal and state level to remain in office, there will be a general bias towards government spending aimed at promoting the welfare of the electorate.

High cost inflation resulting from shortages of oil and other materials in the world at large serves to worsen the inflationary tendency and to add to governments' problems. In the US the problem is intensified in that the use of credit is virtually universal, that is to say, the US consumer has come to rely heavily on access to consumer credit not only for infrequent purchases of consumer durables but for a large part of his daily needs. Thus the credit 'habit' has added to the problem of controlling money and ultimately of curbing price inflation. A determined attack on the problem of inflation which blocked all credit expansion would have an acute effect on the general level of purchasing power, drive the economy into a recession and force up the level of unemployment to extreme levels.

To resist built-in inflationary pressures requires a deliberate set of policies which will unavoidably create the social problems and tensions arising from large-scale unemployment. Those problems are made much worse where, as in the US, unemployment is concentrated more heavily among the young and the coloured sections of the population.

Priorities

Governments, therefore, and not only that of the US, are placed in somewhat of a dilemma in establishing priorities. The crude choice appears to be between price inflation and unemployment. Yet one of the virtues of the democratic system is its ability to reflect popular opinion and pressures.

There can be no doubt of the immense unpopularity of high rates of price inflation. It distorts decision-taking and leads to a preference for tangible assets such as real estate which contribute little to the growth of the productive economy. It reduces the willingness of the businessman to take risks. It is socially unjust in that it penalizes the aged and weaker members of society who are poorly placed to protect their incomes from the erosion of inflation: past savings and thrift are reduced in value.

The general awareness of these problems and the growing dislike of their consequences have produced a revulsion to price inflation which is at length being reflected in government policies. Those policies, presumably endorsed by the electorate, must succeed to some extent. Indeed, if one government fails it is probable that a change in government will not lead to the abandonment of the attempt to cut price inflation; on the contrary, policies may be reinforced. What we do not know, however, is how far electorates are prepared to go with their governments in curbing inflation should the resultant recessions lead to unemployment levels approaching those of the 1930s.

In this respect we do not know what would be tolerated. For one thing, living standards have advanced to such an extent that a person on unemployment relief today probably has a level of purchasing power higher than the national average of 1930s. The average standard of living is roughly three times greater today than in the 1930s. As a result the 'social conscience' with regard to unemployment is probably far less active now than it was at that time. The degree of sympathy for the unemployed is much less as a result of the rise in living standards. Moreover, where priorities are concerned, the growing army of pensioners in society will see their best interests served by a persistent policy aimed at cutting inflation rather than policies aimed at cutting unemployment.

This may be to take an over-cynical view of society at large and will certainly not reflect the views of important minorities. The degree of frustration and deprivation arising from large-scale unemployment must result in protest. Protest today takes a far more violent form than in the 1930s and may well reach such a pitch that public pressures force policy changes on governments. What seems likely is that a general level of unemployment of around 10% will be reached in the US in the 1980–1981 recession. The potential labour force is increasing at more than 1% per annum, so that even with output growth in the economy as a whole in line with the trend in labour productivity (i.e. output per man per year), unemployment would rise. With a fall in total output and with continued increases in output per man year for those people at work, unemployment would rise that much faster.

An *average* level of unemployment of 10% will include some ten million people. Youth unemployment would tend to average 20% across the nation with far higher levels in some areas and extreme levels among the unskilled coloured sections of the population. If the choice is between decelerating inflation and accelerating unemployment, what compromise will be reached as the social tensions mount?

The US potential

To an outside observer, the US appears to possess an enviable reservoir of resources. Her natural resources are such that even the energy problem seems capable of solution. The sources of raw energy are plentiful and the likelihood is that the ingenuity of the research worker, the scientist and technician will devise new ways of producing, converting and transmitting energy on a sufficient scale to make the energy problem a thing of the past. Because of the scale of investment required and the length of time before such investment comes fully into operation, those solutions will take shape late in the 1980s, through the 1990s and into the first decade of the next century.

Similarly, the US possesses a wide range of other mineral resources and a sufficiently fertile agricultural land to endow her with a degree of self-sufficiency denied to most other countries. However, what is perhaps of greater importance still, the people of the US possess a stock of skills—an investment in education—which provides the means of solving not only production problems but also the social problems arising from the attempts to master price inflation. Lest this view be considered over-optimistic and starry-eyed, the successes of the past must be cited in evidence. The massive generation of armaments in the Second World War, the far-sighted and abundant aid to other countries in the recovery period after that war, the lengthy period of low price inflation and an ordered world foreign exchange system, are testimonies to the energy and ingenuity of the US. Perhaps years of fat living have softened the people of the US to the point where the new challenge will not be met successfully. Nevertheless the diversity of the nation and its inherent skills and blend of self-interest must make it extremely imprudent to forecast that the US will fail in the attempt to master inflation.

The range of possibilities must be extremely wide. In the slump of the 1930s, for example, the average price level fell. Between 1929 and 1933, prices dropped by an average of 7.7% per annum. There must be a slim outside chance of something similar recurring. At the other extreme, each wave of price inflation could move higher, each business cycle producing more extreme inflation rates. The ultimate point could be a collapse of the currency, adding to the world's catalogue of such events or, more modestly, high inflation rates could become institutionalized in a way of life where the public learns to live with, and to tolerate, a permanent state of high price inflation.

Within this wide range of possibilities, there is a more probable range of outcome compatible with what we know about US society today. Thus, setting aside the extreme boundaries of possible outcomes to the price system, we now examine current trends, pressures and political possibilities.

The inflationary trends

To set the US performance in context, we must examine the record of money and price inflation for other industrial countries. So far as world prices are concerned, *Chart 6.1* shows consumer price changes from 1950 to 1980 accelerating at about ¼% per annum as a long-term trend[1]. The peak of 10% per annum in the Korean War was followed by a peak of 15% in 1974.

When we examine the course of monetary growth for industrial countries, there was a persistent and accelerating growth from low rates of increase in the

[1]*International Monetary Fund Statistics Yearbook:* consumer prices and money.

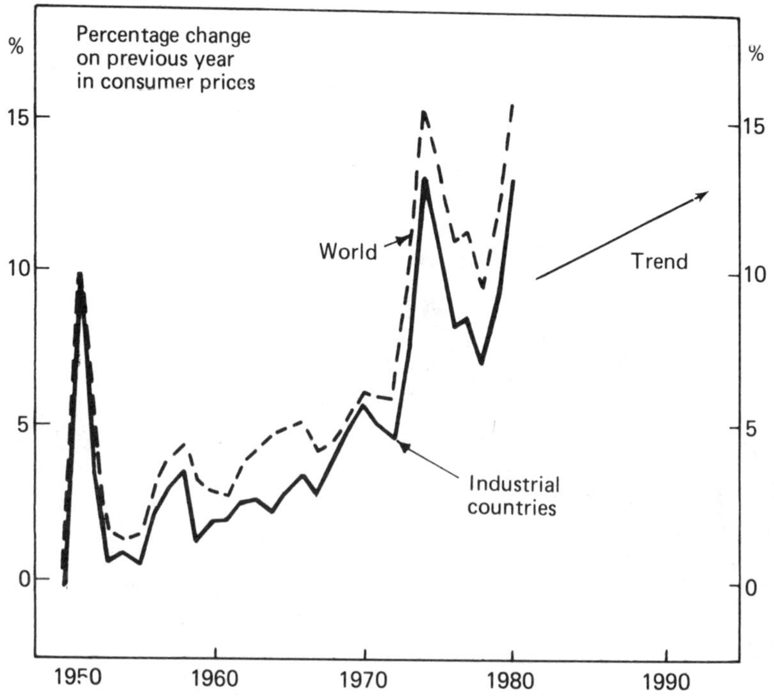

Chart 6.1 World inflation from 1950

1950s (after the Korean War upsurge) to a peak in 1971–1972. This peak occurred ahead of the oil price explosion and the peak in consumer price inflation came in 1974–1975.

Another feature of the relationship between money and prices is illustrated in *Chart 6.2* showing changes in money and consumer prices for the industrialized countries from 1950. Price inflation in the 1950s and 1960s was lower than the rate of money increase. This is explained by the growth in output. In other words, the excess of money growth over output growth showed through in price inflation.

With output growth likely to be lower in the 1980s than in the period to 1973, the gap between money growth and price inflation will be narrower. Thus, although the trend in money growth seems certain to be downwards, the prospective rate of price increase will be closer to the rate of money increase than in the past, probably lagging behind the decline in money growth by about two years. There appears to be, therefore, a fair chance that money growth and price inflation will gradually decline in the industrial countries of the West from the inflation peak of 1980.

The monetary analysis needs to be treated with caution: first, because monetary statistics are difficult to collect and interpret, and secondly since attempts to control money as defined by specific measures, such as cash and current bank deposits (M_1), or M_1 plus time deposits (M_2, M_3, etc), has resulted in changes in performance of the money measures being 'controlled'. This is for the obvious reason that banks and businesses operating under such a system change methods of operation to minimize the effects of the controls on their operations and profitability.

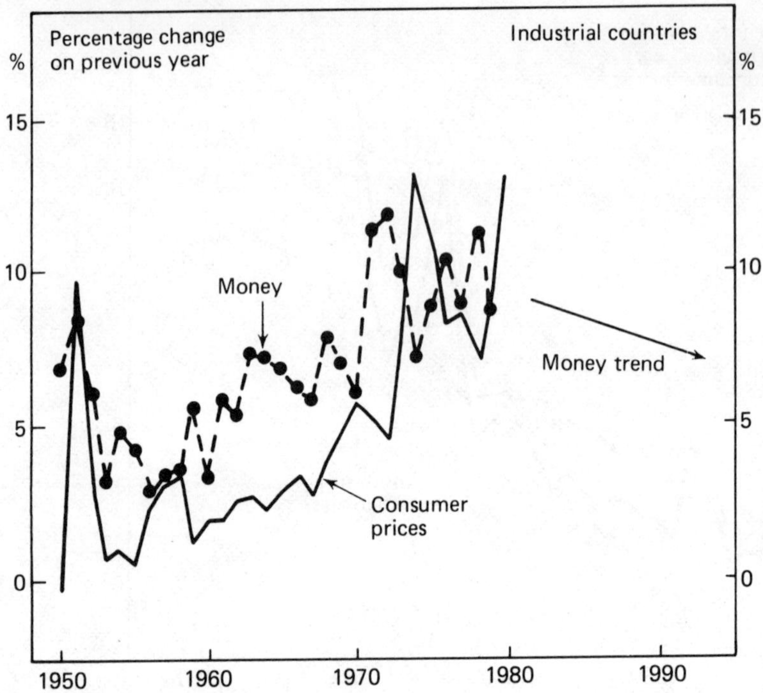

Chart 6.2 Money and inflation

It was the failure of price inflation to 'respond' to close 'regulation' of the money supply in the US that ultimately led to the adoption of specific limits on credit expansion in the US in 1980. We contend that these measures will prove more effective in future and that restricted US money growth will from this point act more positively in curbing future US price inflation.

The problem of money control and prices in the US is illustrated in *Chart 6.3* for money and inflation in the US since 1950. Whereas there was a cosy relationship between money growth and prices for much of the period from 1950, from the mid-1970s price inflation has increased far beyond what might have been expected from money growth on the previous relationship. Indeed, one US analyst, representative of a fairly wide school, published as recently as 1978 the results of a model linking US money (M_1) changes and consumer prices with a ten quarter time-lag, which predicted price inflation at about half the ultimate outturn for 1980[2]. What has gone wrong is that credit expansion has not been adequately reflected in the M_1 series.

Indeed, price inflation in both the US and the UK has been in excess of what might have been anticipated from the previous rates of growth in money supply. The inadequacy of the money measures and control of monetary inflation may very well lie in the expansion of the Eurocurrency markets, outlined in Chapter 4, in which the two countries have been the leading operators.

Moreover, the monetary statistics for Japan and Germany show far larger

[2]BERMAN, P.I. (1978). The Basic Cause of Inflation. *Across the Board* (May 1978) and *Inflation and Money Supply in the United States — 1956–1977*. Lexington Books, Mass.

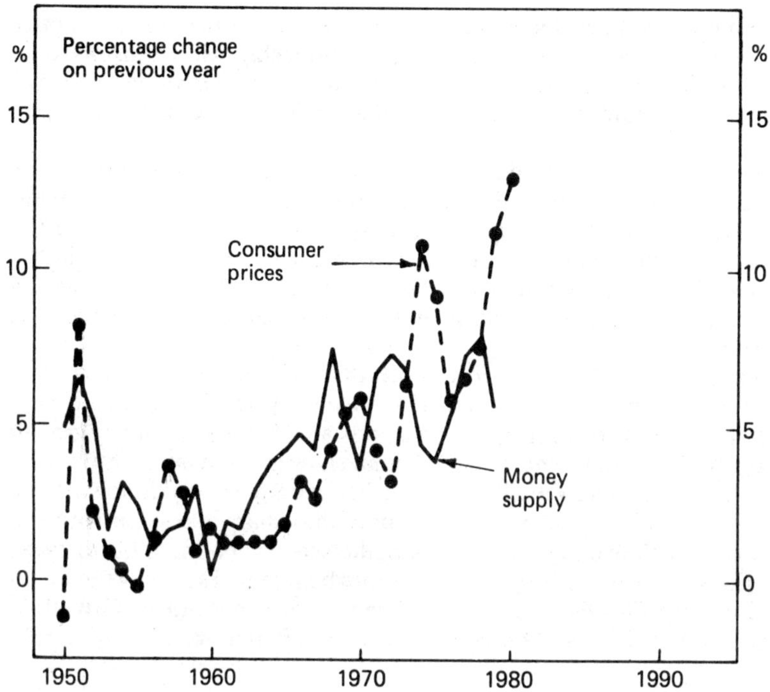

Chart 6.3 US money and inflation

rates of increase in relation to price inflation than in the US and the UK. The banking systems of the two pairs of countries are quite different; add to this the historic role of sterling and the dollar as reserve currencies and it seems likely that monetary control has been exercised far more effectively in Germany and Japan than in the US and the UK.

The comparisons shown in the following *Table 6.1* of 'surplus' money and price inflation for the six-year cycle ending in 1980 illustrate the argument. The excess of money growth over output growth can be taken as a proxy for

Table 6.1 Money and inflation

	1972–1978 (% per annum)					1974–1980 (% per annum)
	Money Growth*	÷	*Output Growth*	=	*Surplus Money Growth*	*Change in Consumer prices*
Industrial countries	9.3		3.2		5.9	9.5
USA	5.9		3.0		2.8	9.1
Germany	9.6		2.4		7.0	4.5
Japan	15.5		4.7		10.3	7.5
Switzerland	4.2		nil		4.2	3.1
UK	12.3		2.1		10.0	16.0

*Money year end to year end of previous year; other series are annual averages
Source: IMF Financial Statistics Yearbook

'surplus' money growth which would tend to generate a matching rate of price inflation with a lag of, say, two years. The relationship will be distorted by changes in the velocity of circulation of money, an increase in volocity tending to finance a faster rate of price inflation than indicated by 'surplus' money growth.

The averages for all industrial countries in the IMF classification show price inflation of 9½% per annum against surplus money growth of 6% per annum. We contend that this discrepancy reflects some degree of increase in the velocity of circulation and also an understatement of money growth in the series in question. The average will have been heavily influenced by the US statistics within the industrial total and, to a lesser extent, by the UK performance.

In the case of the US, prices rose more than 6% per annum more than indicated by surplus money and in the UK the 'excess' price rise was of the same order. Yet in Germany prices rose *less* than indicated by surplus money growth falling short by 2½% per annum, while Japan showed a similar performance. By contrast, Switzerland actually reduced her money supply following the surge in prices in 1974, pushing the economy into sharp recession with the result that output showed no increase over the six-year period 1972 to 1978. Price inflation dropped to 1% per annum before being lifted again by the world oil price rises of 1979–1980 and the associated rise in other prices. Growth in surplus money and the resultant consumer price inflation were fairly closely related.

Exchange rates and inflation

An important feature in checking cost and price inflation in Switzerland, Germany and Japan in the period to 1980 was the strength of the currency in those countries in relation to the rest of the world, and particularly the US dollar and the pound sterling. It will be recognized that the lower a country's cost and price inflation compared with a competing country, the more will the currency of that country appreciate against the higher inflation competitor. This, of course, assumes that exchange rates are determined in the long-run by considerations of purchasing power parity.

The theory of purchasing power parity has a forceful logic. Higher comparative cost movements will reduce the profitability of exports, weaken export competitiveness and strengthen import competitiveness. This will be reflected in a lower market share and a deteriorating current account balance of payments. The latter will be reflected in supply and demand movements in the exchange markets which will tend to depress the exchange rate of the higher inflation country. This will make the cost of imports greater, thus importing an added element of cost and price inflation.

All of this may take some two years or so to filter through the cost/price system, although it should be stressed that since the cost and price inflation statistics are generally available for all to see with a time lag of only a few weeks, relative inflation rates between countries are known well in advance of the ultimate effects of those differentials on trade and commerce. Therefore, the *expectation* of change in performance will tend to be reflected ahead of the ultimate impact of the inflation differentials on the current account balance of payments. The exchange rate may, therefore, move against the high inflation country in anticipation of the change. Such movements can be frustrated to a limited extent by official intervention. A government may attempt to 'buy time' by using reserves, or raising foreign loans, to support the exchange rate while adopting domestic policies aimed at forcing down the domestic rate of cost and price inflation, in order to restore the competitive position. By and large, governments have not succeeded and in spite of high interest rates short-term capital has tended to move out.

The purchasing power parity theory is similar to the monetary approach to exchange rate analysis[3]. Differences between countries in respect of rates of money growth in relation to output (i.e. surplus money or 'real' money growth) lead to the sequence of pressures outlined above and to changes in exchange rates.

What will be apparent from this analysis is that we have an example of the 'rich getting richer while the poor get poorer'. The virtuous lower inflation country will enjoy an appreciating exchange rate and a lower rate of import price inflation, while the reverse will be the case for the above-average inflation country. This feature undoubtedly contributed to differences in money and inflation performances between Germany, Japan and Switzerland on the one side and the US and the UK on the other. For every winner there has to be a loser.

Future rates of inflation will thus be determined in part by relative performance between countries in so far as this influences the respective exchange rates. That being said, the balance of payments features remain dominant, as is exemplified by the effects of price changes on payments debits and credits resulting from key movements in the oil market. Countries almost entirely dependent on oil imports, such as Germany, Japan, France and Italy, have seen soaring import bills forcing their current account payments positions into deficit. This feature has been reflected in exchange rate movements. In parallel, the UK, now a net oil exporter, has seen sterling priced well above the level indicated by the UK's purchasing power parity. Another example is the effect of the high price of gold on South Africa's payments and the value of the rand in the exchange markets.

These features have to be assessed so far as future inflation is concerned. The prospects for the dollar and the leading currencies will hinge not only on money supply considerations but on developments, particularly in the field of energy, bearing on the oil import bills of the industrial countries.

Future inflation

As we have seen, a variety of pressures has led to accelerating rates of price inflation throughout the late 1960s and 1970s. In the first place, money growth increased, mainly in response to US financing of the Vietnam War and to attempts to ward off recession in the early 1970s and to check the growth in unemployment. Soaring oil and commodity prices then imparted a violent acceleration in cost and price inflation and this was accommodated to some extent by faster rises in money expansion, again aimed at reducing the depressing impact of rising energy costs.

[3]SAVILLE, I.D. (March 1980). The Sterling Dollar rate in the Floating Rate Period: the Role of Money, Prices and Intervention. *Bank of England Discussion Paper No. 9*. London.

With the second wave of oil price rises, growing concern at the problem of price inflation led to an attempt on the part of the US to exercise more effective control over money. With the BIS expressing concern at the need to restrain the growth of the Euromarket, the other central bank members of the BIS are also likely to tighten domestic money control.

What this suggests is that money growth will be less inflationary in the 1980s than in the 1970s, even allowing for continued slow growth in world output. From a peak in 1980, average price inflation of the industrialized countries is likely to decline erratically from one business cycle to the next. This view is reinforced by the likelihood of a moderation in oil price rises. Although we argue that the imbalance in the world's energy markets will persist and that oil prices will rise by around an average of 4–5% per annum more than consumer prices in the 1980s, the gradual solution of the energy problem will lead to a lower rate of cost inflation.

Nevertheless, the inherent pressures towards inflation in the democratic countries will persist and concern over mounting unemployment will create difficulties in holding down government spending, government fiscal deficits and money growth. To counter this problem it may be that institutional arrangements aimed at curbing wage and price increases and minimizing inflationary expectations will be strengthened. The public 'will' to correct inflation will lend support to public measures of this kind, whatever their shortcomings.

It will also be the case that the respective balance of payments of the leading countries will be different in the 1980s from those in the 1970s. The US is unlikely to expand her economy, regardless of the payments consequences, as she did in the 1970s. Her payments position, in surplus in 1980, seems more likely to be on average in balance on current account throughout the 1980s for the first time since the immediate post-war period. With the likelihood of a declining oil import bill as a proportion of total imports and a net inflow of capital, the dollar seems likely to recover from its undervalued position and this would contribute to a small extent to easing domestic cost and price inflation. Japan and Germany, on the other hand, are more likely to be in a different position. The inherent strength of their balance of payments has been reduced and their currencies will not perform with the same force *vis à vis* the dollar. It will be relatively more difficult, therefore, for those countries to utilize currency appreciation as a check on internal price inflation. The gap in performance will narrow.

There are limits to this potential change, however, arising from the respective rates of investment ploughback and productivity growth of the three economies. Japan and Germany have far higher investment ploughback rates than the US. As a result, their prospective productivity gains, paring the rate of cost increase, will be higher than that of the US. The chances are, therefore, that cost and price inflation will be higher in the US, though the differential will be tending to narrow compared with the 1970s.

In the short-run, the US is making a belated attempt to raise energy prices more closely in line with world prices. In contrast to other industrialized oil-importing countries, where oil and other energy prices were moved up to reflect world oil price rises, the US held back in the mid-1970s, keeping her energy cost inflation well below the world average. In 1979-1980 US oil prices were adjusted upwards, leading to a sharper rate of cost inflation; but her energy prices were still below the world average, suggesting future US energy price rises could well be greater than those of competing countries.

However, the attempts of the US to curb inflation should not be belittled. Central government spending in the US as a share of GNP is appreciably lower than the average for industrial Europe. Similarly, the central government fiscal deficits in the US seem likely to be held to a low average of 1% of GNP compared with around 4% for industrial Europe. Allowing for the time-lags between cost and price increases, US price inflation seems likely to come down more quickly in the early 1980s than in other countries.

Another important historical feature is that price inflation has either been reversed or reduced in each of the recessions in the 200-year history of the US. Clearly the 1980-1981 recession is unlikely to prove an exception. How far and how fast the process of cutting inflation proceeds will be determined by a complex of factors, not least success or failure in re-stimulating productive investment. In this connection a cautionary note was sounded by Michael E. Levy in a study presented at the 1979 Professors' Conference in St. Louis which was summarized as follows[4]:

> Successful inflation control depends on removal of the fundamental causes of US inflation. Fiscal and monetary policy restraint, while necessary, will not be sufficient. New policies to encourage greater productive efforts and faster real growth will be essential, if price stability is to be restored in the 1980s.
>
> In essence, we must redirect economic policy from a consumption economy propelled by 'social activism' to a production economy, from regulation that impedes efficiency to stimulation of research and development, from rewarding mainly *non-producing* consumers to rewarding producers, investors and risk-takers. Politically, we have failed utterly in achieving even a modest reorientation along these lines during the last 15 years, and I can see no compelling reason why we would succeed better right now.

This view was reinforced in an analysis and historical view by Ashby Bladen[5], pinpointing the critical role of credit in financing inflation. His comments summarizing inflationary pressures in the US are as follows:

> Once we recognize clearly that all the things that get lent and spent in modern economies are financial instruments, which are promises to repay in exchange for then-current purchasing power, and that there no longer exists any limit to the ability of the financial system to create financial claims corresponding to the limit that was imposed upon the financial systems of the nineteenth century by the creditors' ability to exchange financial instruments for money that possessed intrinsic value, it is easy to see why inflation has become such an intractable problem. First, most of us are more fond of the purchasing power than we are of the work that is involved in earning it by producing real goods and services. Second, in political democracies the way to get elected to political office is to promise the people more of the unearned

[4]LEVY, M.E. (April 1980). Guns and a Little Margarine Too. *Across the Board.* New York.
[5]BLADEN, A. (1980). How to cope with the Developing Financial Crisis. *Across the Board.* New York.

> purchasing power that can be created by the apparently magical and effortless process of debt formation than your opponent does. Third, social democracy asserts that incomes are deserved as a matter of right whether or not we produce real goods and services; and the only way that incomes can be produced out of thin air, without the effort and bother of producing real goods and services, is through debt formation—at the cost of inflation. Finally, once practical people grasp the implications of all this and decide that inflation is here to stay, they rush to borrow as heavily as they can in order to buy real things whose prices they hope will at least keep up with the inflation. Thus a self-sustaining spiral is generated that has the capacity to continue and to accelerate indefinitely as long as credit remains generally available. Once inflation has become endemic, the *only* sure way to stop it is to limit the creation of new credit to the amount that is likely to be used for real productive investment.

We contend, however, that the moves taken by the Federal Reserve since this passage was written give hope that the necessary curbs to credit growth will lower the prospective rate of money and price inflation and that some, at least of the lessons of the inflationary past have been learned.

The problem of inflation and the possible remedies were outlined by Henry C. Wallich, a member of the Board of Governors of the Federal Reserve System in an address in 1979[6].

> Inflation is so universally damaging, why is it that we have made so little headway against it? In particular, why is it that in the year in which the government made the fight against inflation its number one priority, inflation has once more accelerated into the double-digit range? The basic reason, I believe, is that in fighting inflation we are still violating the first rule of economics: that there is no such thing as a free lunch. We delude ourselves if we believe that a cure will not be painful and costly. But the ultimate pain and cost of letting inflation go on is far greater. There is no way of 'living with inflation'. Unattended, it will accelerate in the future as it has done in the past, contrary to many predictions, and will end up by destroying our market economy.
>
> What we shall have to do, in broadest terms, is this:
>
> (1) Allow for somewhat greater slack in the economy in the form of more excess capacity and unemployment than we would ordinarily want to accept. We must reject speculative calculations of the amount of output that we would be sacrificing by such a policy. That additional output would never be available in an economy wracked by inflation as ours is. At the same time, we must continue to compensate decently those who, for shorter or longer periods, suffer unemployment. We can immediately reduce the worse part of our unemployment, that of teenagers, by lifting temporarily or, better, premanently the minimum wage restrictions that militate against employment of teenagers.
>
> (2) We must end the many activities of the Federal government that spawn inflation, including numerous forms of regulation.

[6]WALLICH, H.C. (August 1979). The Inflation Syndrome. *Across the Board.* New York. An article from an address given to a meeting sponsored by Westminster College to the Chamber of Commerce, Ogden, Utah.

(3) We must bring government expenditures under better control. While I do not believe that a constitutional amendment for an ever-balanced budget is a practical answer, we can and should set firm limits on government expenditure.
(4) We should pursue a strong anti-inflationary monetary policy, taking advantage of the fact that, while monetary policy works only with a lag on employment and output, its effect on prices, which works by affecting people's expectations, can be much quicker.
(5) We should implement guidelines of the kind established by the President and support them, together with a real wage guarantee or some other use of the tax system to restrain the wage-price spiral.
(6) We should reform the tax system to strengthen our productive forces and eliminate the existing bias against productive activities.

The execution of such a policy would have to take many forms. It will encounter resistance and will require courage and steadfastness. I have no doubt that the solution to the problem of inflation is in our hands. The cost of victory in this struggle may be high, but the cost of losing would be incalculable.

We must also recognize the fact that the dominant position of the US in the world economy means that the US has a critical role to play in the attempt to curb inflation. The fact that total output of the US accounts for nearly 40% of the output of the free world economies means that any strong upsurge in spending and demand in the US must have its impact on supplies and prices in other countries. Conversely, a downturn in the US will reduce demand for raw materials and commodities as well as for manufactured goods of other countries. Thus, deflationary policies in the US will contribute to a lowering of price inflation through its impact on world commodity markets.

The determination of the US, therefore, to moderate its own inflation will serve to reduce inflationary pressures elsewhere in the world. In addition, the labour position in the US is markedly different from that in other western countries. Because of the below-average age of her population the structure of the workforce is different. There are more young people entering the labour force in the US year by year than there are older people leaving it through retirement. The implication of this situation is that the supply of labour in the US should tend to result in a lower level of wage inflation than in Europe. Since the US is the dominant force in the world economy and will tend to be a pace-setter so far as efforts to curb inflation are concerned, the fact of lower wage pressures in the US should help other countries in their efforts to check inflation.

Drawing the various strands in the argument together, we forecast a declining rate of price inflation for the US in the 1980s and a gradual closing of the gap between her own rate of price inflation and that of Japan and Germany. We would expect the US inflation rate to be below that of other industrial countries. The range of inflation forecasts is illustrated in *Chart 6.4*.

It will probably take as long for price inflation to decline as it did to accelerate. Indeed, the obstacles to curbing inflation suggest that the process will take longer. We take the view, however, that having glimpsed the abyss opened up by accelerating price inflation, the people and governments of the

US and the advanced industrial economies are prepared to accept the discomforts required to arrest and curb inflation and to establish over time more secure mechanics of credit management aimed to limit price inflation to the average rates of the 1950s and 1960s. Such an objective may not be attainable until the 1990s.

Although the boundaries of the US inflation forecasts are drawn rather widely, the potential trend from one business cycle to the next is expected to show a decline of between ⅓ to 1% per annum. Within each cycle, price inflation will probably vary from year to year producing a range of up to 6% between high and low years. These cyclical extremes are included in the forecast range for inflation shown in *Chart 6.4*.

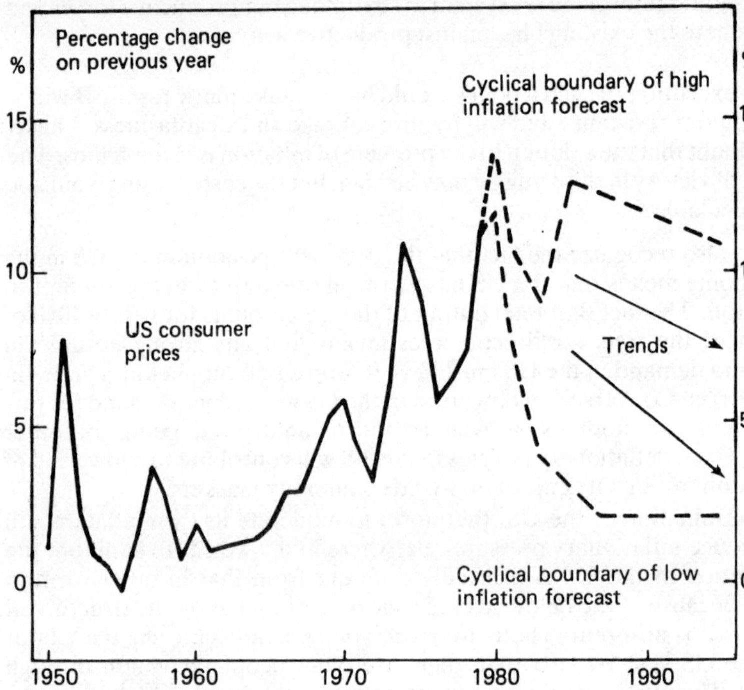

Chart 6.4 Future inflation

To summarize our expectations, the gap between the inflation rate of the US and the rest of the industrial world is likely to close fairly rapidly—say, by 1982. The gap between the US and Germany will take longer to close and such a goal seems attainable in the second half of the 1980s. By then the US inflation rate will probably be lower than the average for the other western industrial economies. Against such a scenario, the recovery in the dollar would be significant. However, among all the other possible prospects for the future, the involvement of the US in war in one form or another would have different consequences, both for inflation and the dollar.

The implications of such forecasts for the future role of the dollar are considered in conjunction with the future world economic power structure and developments in the Eurocurrency and foreign exchange markets in assessing prospects for the world currency and reserve system. We now turn to examine the future world economic power structure.

7

Changes in the world economic power structure

The importance of a national economy in terms of world production and trade has an obvious bearing on the use of that country's currency in international transactions. Where one country achieves a dominant economic position, as was the case with the UK in the nineteenth century, not only will its currency be extensively used in world commerce, but the prospects are that it will also be used as a world reserve asset.

This has been the position of the US and the dollar in the twentieth century. Although the US share of world trade since the Second World War has not matched the share achieved by the UK in her heyday, the sheer size of the US economy and its output has inevitably contributed to the development of the dollar as a world reserve currency. Because of the strength and attractiveness of the dollar in the immediate post-war period, the currency achieved its status as the most common unit of account in the transactions of the free world economy. Thus it was not so much the share of world trade enjoyed by the US which contributed to the reserve role of the dollar, but rather the expansion of world commerce and the use of the dollar by other countries. It was also the rapid growth of the international capital markets, as well as the changes in the oil markets, which contributed to the dominant position of the dollar as a reserve asset. The great increases in oil prices in the 1970s, with oil priced in dollar terms, led to the accumulation of still larger dollar balances in the hands of oil producers and strengthened the relative importance of the dollar and dollar transactions as a share of world commercial activity.

In exploring the future of the US dollar and the world reserve system it is therefore appropriate to examine the likely changes in the future world economic power structure and to raise the question whether the dominance of the US in the world economy will be eclipsed just as the UK dominance was eclipsed earlier in the twentieth century.

The economic power structure of the 1970s

In the 1970s the total output of the US economy accounted for nearly a quarter of world output. The relative importance of the major economies and groupings is shown in *Table 7.1*.

Table 7.1 World output by main countries and groups, 1975

	Approximate weights (%)
US	23
Canada	3½
Japan	10½
Germany	7
France	6
UK	4½
Italy	3½
Belgium	1
Netherlands	1
USSR and Eastern Europe	20
India	3
China	3½
Others	13½
World Total	100
of which:	
OECD	61
EEC	24

Source: United Nations Annual Statistics

It will be seen that US output in 1975 was more than twice as great as that of Japan, the second largest producer within the western world. Even the USSR and the communist countries of Eastern Europe together accounted for a smaller share of world output than the US and, if the comparison is limited to the countries of the OECD, the US still accounts for nearly 40% of total output. Because of its greater degree of self-sufficiency than other countries, America's share of world trade is less than its share of output. During the 1970s her share in volume terms averaged around 18% while Japan, where trade was growing more rapidly, accounted for some 7% of the world's total. Japan, too, has a lesser dependence on international trade than the countries of western Europe, so that even with faster growth rates, it would be many years before Japanese trade accounted for a share of the world total equal to that of the US.

For the purposes of this analysis the Russian bloc can be excluded since the chances of communist expansion to the point where the Russian rouble becomes a world currency must be regarded as extremely slight. Therefore, in assessing the future trends of world output and commerce, from the point of view of the world's exchange and reserve system, the analysis has to be concerned with the relative rates of expansion of the US economy alongside the leading western economies.

The dramatic slowdown in world output growth during the 1970s did little to change the relative importance and performance of the western economies. From 1973, when the combination of oil price rises and accelerating price inflation interrupted world output growth, economic performance has changed fundamentally compared with the period of rapid expansion over the previous generation. The factors contributing to that slowdown are varied. In the first place, the sharp increases in oil prices have served to reduce purchasing power for non-oil items. Energy cost increases have reduced business and consumer purchasing power. Growing concern at the problem of price inflation has led the western economies to adopt restrictive policies which, in turn, have curbed the growth in spending power.

Perhaps of greater importance, we should recognize that the fast growth of investment throughout the post-war period gradually contributed to an accumulation of capital on such a scale that surplus capacity became a prominent feature in the great majority of world industries. This stage of capital saturation had been reached by the 1970s and it was inevitable that lower rates of growth in investment spending would follow regardless of the changes inflicted by the rise in oil prices. Associated with the decline in the rate of investment, world trade in manufactured goods expanded at a far more modest pace. Since investment goods enter into world trade to a considerable extent, the investment slowdown inevitably resulted in a slowdown in international trade.

Thus, the change in direction of investment and trade together reduced the rate of growth in world demand to such an extent as to halve the rate of growth in total output. The 1970s, therefore, witnessed a transformation of world economic performance both in terms of output and trade. Thus, from this point of time in 1980, the factors tending to limit the rate of growth in output and trade are particularly powerful and prospects for the 1980s at least are for slower rates of growth in output than in the post-war period up to 1973.

Prospects for the 1980s

World output growth has roughly halved since 1973. Over the previous 20 years, growth in the OECD group of countries averaged 4½% per annum, whereas between 1973 and 1979 (comparable years in terms of the world business cycle) output growth averaged 2¼% per annum. The factors responsible for this reduction in the rate of expansion are just as powerful in the early 1980s as in the mid-1970s.

There are eight main factors likely to determine the rate of world output growth in the 1980s. These are:

(1) Capital saturation, leading to low investment growth in the first half of the decade.
(2) Above average rises in oil prices, tending to reduce spending power for non-oil items.
(3) Counter-inflation policies, reducing spending throughout the first half of the decade.
(4) Protectionism, motivated by the need to reduce dependence on outside supplies and to limit unemployment, tending to reduce growth in world trade throughout the decade.
(5) Counter-unemployment policies later in the decade, tending to increase output growth.
(6) Increased defence spending, motivated by growing world uncertainty, particularly with regard to sources of essential supplies, likely to contribute to output growth throughout the decade.
(7) The search for new sources of energy, and research and investment into

improved forms of energy production and transmission as well as economies in the use of energy which will all tend to increase spending and output.

(8) The impact of the electronics revolution and technical change in terms of investment, tending to expand spending and output throughout the decade.

While the first four of these factors will exert a contractionary influence on output growth as a whole, the last four will work in the opposite direction. It is not necessarily the case that the two sets of factors will cancel out so far as their impact on demand and output is concerned. If that were the case it could be argued that economic performance in the 1980s will be no different from performance since 1973. On balance this seems highly probable with the reservation that output growth could well be lower in the first half of the decade. The main reason for such an assumption lies in the factors making for high unemployment round the world, and the probable response to that problem later in the decade.

The major cause of rising unemployment is the increase in young people entering the labour force over the numbers of older people retiring. In the advanced industrial countries the birthrate accelerated to produce a baby boom in the late 1950s and early 1960s. The birthrate peaked at a relatively high level in the 1960s, with the result that the numbers of young people entering the potential labour force from school and university rose during the second half of the 1970s, and will continue to do so in a pronounced way in the first half of the 1980s. While this is a characteristic of the advanced countries, it is no less the case that in the poorer developing countries, where birthrates have been at higher levels in any case, the supply of potential labour will continue to rise.

Some idea of the magnitude of the problem can be seen from the labour statistics for the US. The population age structure is relatively young compared with northern Europe, and the natural increase in the size of the labour force in the US will be about 1½% per annum in the early years of the 1980s. This implies that employment has to rise by around one and a half millions a year simply to prevent unemployment rising further. While the problem is not so severe in the countries of northern Europe where the age structure is somewhat older, nevertheless the problem of making sufficient new employment opportunities will remain acute.

The whole problem of mounting unemployment is likely to be exacerbated by other factors. In the first instance the generally low levels of profitability and business confidence have resulted in a determination by many large employers to economize in the use of labour. A high proportion of new investment in the 1970s was concentrated on labour savings. In any case, replacement investment is always likely to give higher plant capacity and to offer further scope for economies of labour.

It may also be the case that this tendency will be reinforced through the impact of the electronics revolution. The pace of technical change in this field continues to be so rapid that new generations of equipment at relatively low cost may well lead to faster changes in productive systems which seem certain to reduce labour requirements. The growth of robotic systems of manufacturing production will result in fewer people being required on the factory floor while similar economies are likely in some branches of the service industries. There will be some counter-weight to this as investment and output increase in the electronics sector itself, and as the new technologies generate new forms of service activities. On balance, however, it seems probable that the new technical revolution will lead to a net loss of employment.

A further factor in the advanced countries is that the continuing drive towards female equality, as well as the tougher economic conditions, have contributed to the swing towards an extremely low birthrate. This feature correlates with the rising proportion of women at work, and the evidence suggests that the proportion of women wishing to join the labour force will tend to rise in the 1980s.

These factors combine to produce a potential unemployment problem on a scale not witnessed since the 1930s. Indeed, the recession at the outset of the 1980s seems likely to drive unemployment levels around the world to the point where unemployment becomes a dominant political issue. For this reason it seems prudent to assume that government policies will gradually be adjusted during the 1980s in a more expansionary direction. An important influence in this respect seems likely to be growing concern about youth unemployment. Unemployment among young people in the industrialized countries is about twice as great as the average rate of unemployment. With the tendency for youth unemployment to go higher still, the resultant social pressures are likely sooner or later to result in political action.

In the short-run, spending and output growth are being restricted not only by the impact of the surge in oil and energy prices, but in the general attempt to curb inflation. Restrictive monetary policies are likely to continue in force throughout the early 1980s and, as we argued in a previous chapter, monetary discipline is likely to revert to a more orthodox and less inflationary pattern from now on. In the early 1980s, however, the effects of cuts in government spending, notably in the US and the UK, linked with more effective controls of money supply, seem certain to damp down output growth with some severity. But assuming such policies meet with some success, the continuance of restraints on money growth would have a less restrictive impact on output growth in the second half of the 1980s.

The same restrictive effect on spending and output must be expected from continued upward pressure on oil prices. The erratic and vulnerable nature of world oil supplies in the 1980s points to continued above-average price rises in spite of the efforts to economize in oil consumption. The net result will probably be a rise in oil prices averaging around 4–5% per annum faster than consumer prices through the 1980s. This would cut spending in real terms on non-energy items by around ½% per annum. High spending by the beneficiaries in the oil exporting world is unlikely to generate a sufficient increase in the imports of those countries to offset the reduction in purchasing power in the rest of the world.

Against this general background it is hardly surprising that the trend is emerging in the world economy towards protectionism. After a phase of remarkable success in the generation after the Second World War in moving towards free trade, progress has now been halted. Although politicians will continue to pay lip service to the virtues of free trade, the evidence is entirely in the opposite direction. Quota and administrative restrictions are on the increase, and although generalized import controls seem unlikely, trade restrictions between the major blocs are expected to increase. Not only are obstacles to trade increasing between the US, the EEC and Japan but

Table 7.2 World output growth 1980–1990

	Approximate weights: 1975	*Growth rates (% per annum)*
US	23	2½–3½
Canada	3½	3 –4
Japan	10½	3½–4½
Germany	7	2 –3
France	6	2½–3½
UK	4½	2 –3
Italy	3½	2 –3
Belgium	1	2 –3
Netherlands	1	2 –3
USSR and Eastern Europe	20	3¼–4¼
India	3	3¼–4¼
China	3½	4¾–5¾
Other	13½	3 –4
World Total	100	3 –4
of which:		
OECD	61	2¾–3¾
EEC	24	2 –3

Source: *Britain through the 1980s*, James Morrell, Gower Publishing, 1980

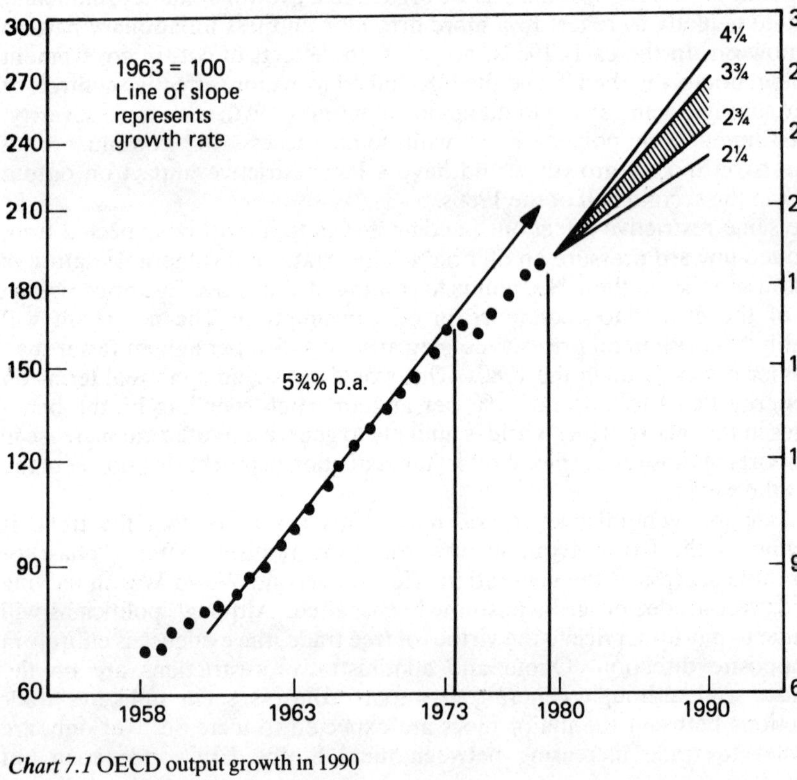

Chart 7.1 OECD output growth in 1990

restrictions are likely to be increasingly imposed against the newly industrializing countries who are successfully undercutting the more mature industrial economies. Thus, the trend towards protectionism seems likely to gather pace in the 1980s, tending to slow world trade increase and, in turn, to hamper output growth.

Summarizing the effects of these various influences, our forecast of world output growth in the 1980s is shown in *Table 7.2*. The forecast shows a prospective average rate of growth for the whole world economy of 3–4% per annum. This is higher than the results achieved in the period between 1973 and 1980 and the basic assumption underlying this aspect of the forecast is that restrictive factors, such as surplus capacity and low investment, ease as the decade progresses, while the restrictive counter-inflation policies give way to expansionary policies aimed at reducing unemployment.

Allowing for the range of uncertainties, the forecast for the OECD group of countries is shown in perspective in *Chart 7.1*.

In contrast to a rate of increase in output of nearly 6% per annum in the 1960s, the growth rate forecast for the 1980s is put between 2¾ and 3¾% per annum with an outside chance of the range being as wide as 2¼–4¼% per annum.

Prospects for the 1990s

With large investment in energy programmes in the 1980s the chances are that the world's energy crisis will begin to fade in the 1990s. A better supply and range of energy and greater economies in energy use should be attainable in the last decade of the century, and this feature should result in a return towards higher rates of spending and output growth. In addition, in the advanced countries the population structure will be different as a result of the low birth-rates of the 1970s. The size of the potential working population may in fact shrink to some extent in the richer countries, while the decline of birthrates worldwide will contribute to a slowing of both total population growth and the rate of increase in the workforce in the developing countries. This feature may make the unemployment problem less urgent, though we suspect governments will still be under pressure to stimulate spending and output growth.

However, there is a wide range of uncertainties surrounding any forecast looking so far ahead. Perhaps the most profound is the prospect of war. Power politics has always rested on the threat of force. Yet the crude use of force has been progressively abandoned at a national scale under the growing influence of the concept of international justice and law and order. There is also the point that growing concern as to where the use of modern weapons of destruction could lead may inhibit the use of those weapons.

Even so, it would be extremely foolish not to recognize that the problems of population growth, scarce resources, rising unemployment, militant Islamism and social unrest constitute a greater threat to the world order and to security than at any time since the 1930s. Throughout the past decade at least violence and terrorism have been steadily increasing, and regional conflicts within many countries are a reminder of the diverse nature of armed conflict as well as the increasing potential for international disputes.

Although we put low odds on conventional war between the US and the USSR, this does not mean that the arms race is likely to be halted. The improvements in technology seem certain to contribute to growth in defence spending at least throughout the 1980s, and this may well be concentrated on the information, or spy, systems of space satellites. A war in space is no longer a fantasy of science fiction and it is quite conceivable that a war between the superpowers could be waged in space with the object of destroying the vital information satellites on which both sides seem to depend. While both the USSR and the US seem likely to draw back from the ultimate provocation of threatening the vital interests of each other, the chances of a nuclear conflict cannot be dismissed entirely, not least through accident or a failure in control systems.

Even though a war of this kind seems a somewhat remote possibility, large scale wars of a different order cannot be ruled out. War between the USSR and China, India and Pakistan and involving states in and bordering on the Middle East are all dangerous possibilities. When we consider that only a small minority of the world's nation states enjoy liberal and democratic government, and that dictatorship or arbitrary government is the more general rule, and that added to this the spread of ownership and control of nuclear power and nuclear weapons is increasing, then the chances of some irresponsible action must be considered to tend to increase with the passage of time.

Although we are inclined to the view that Europe will escape major armed conflict, it seems more probable that regional disruptions and violence will tend to increase. In addition, national uprisings in Eastern Europe, for example, remain a real possibility which could result in general hostilities should the western powers lend support to such rebellions. On balance, however, we put low odds on such a possibility.

Nevertheless, the possibilities of armed conflict still seem likely to increase in the next two decades, with a fairly high chance of a war on the scale of Korea or Vietnam occurring during that period.

Assuming that the prospect of war will increase, the consequences for economic growth in the various regions of the world are hard to predict. One general assumption which seems acceptable is that defence spending, whether directly or not on war, seems certain to increase, thus contributing to economic growth potential. The consequences of war, however, show up in different ways and one likelihood is that their impact on both the demand and availability of raw materials would be significant, thus tending to force up world commodity prices. It may also be the case that world trade would be disrupted and to a greater extent than we have assumed with the growing tendency towards protectionism.

On balance we suspect that the various factors shaping world spending and output will tend towards some improvement in growth rates in the 1990s compared with the 1980s, although this would still result in a lower performance than in the 25 years following the Second World War. In discussing the limits to future growth Rostow[1] analyses various projections made for the long-term future under various headings and reaches fairly sanguine conclusions. It seems certain that the slowing down of world population growth will continue, thus easing the potential problem so far as food supplies are

[1]ROSTOW, W.W. (1978). *The World Economy, History and Prospects*. New York; Macmillan.

concerned. The prospects are less promising with regard to materials and whereas man's ingenuity and investment seem likely to be heavily concentrated in an attempt to find a solution to the energy problem in the 1980s and 1990s, those efforts may well be redirected towards solving the potential shortages of certain key materials in the 1990s and beyond. Nevertheless, problems with material supply seem likely to enhance national attempts to secure a greater degree of economic independence and we should recognize that shortages of materials other than energy could continue to retard output growth in the 1990s. Not least among those problems may be the question of adequate water supplies.

But problems provoke reactions and recent evidence is encouraging in that research and investment seems likely to be a major expansionary force into the 1990s. We can see already not only in the wide field of energy but in electronics and biochemistry that a new phase of world industrial expansion may well be in the making. For these reasons we postulate that there is a reasonable prospect of some acceleration in output growth rates in the 1990s, although with an uneven pattern between countries and groupings. The world economic power structure will be significantly different by the end of the century.

The future world economic power structure

Our forecasts for output growth and the resultant share of world output are summarized in *Table 7.3* for the major world blocs. The main differences in performance are attributable to population factors and material resources. Population growth has already halted in the advanced countries although the US and Japan, having younger age structures than the countries of the EEC as a whole, have the prospect of faster growth in the potential labour force in the 1980s and will, therefore, reach the point of declining population at a later date than the EEC.

Table 7.3 World output growth to the year 2000

	1975 share (%)	*Growth rate 1980–1990 (% per annum)*	*1990 share (%)*	*Growth rate 1990–2000 (% per annum)*	*2000 share (%)*
US	23.0	2.5 –3.5	21.4	2.5 –4	20.4
Canada	3.5	3 –4	3.5	3 –4.5	3.5
US and Canada	26.5		24.9		23.9
EEC	24	2 –3	20.7	2 –3.5	18.8
Japan	10.5	3.5–4.5	11.3	3.5–5	11.8
OECD	61	2.75–3.75	58.8	2.75–4.25	57.4
World	100	3 –4	100.0	3 –4.5	100.0

Of perhaps greater importance so far as output growth potential is concerned, the EEC is the economic bloc with the biggest energy problem. The UK apart, the EEC countries are almost entirely dependent on imported oil, whereas the US has a far higher degree of self-sufficiency and in the long run must be regarded as potentially self-sufficient in energy resources. The same

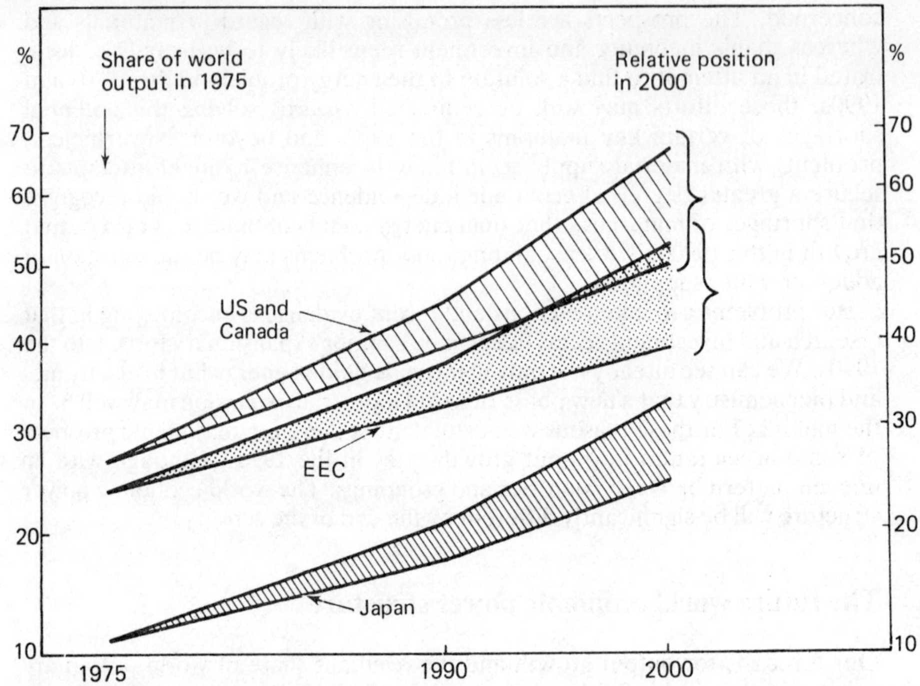

Chart 7.2 Output growth to 2000

comparisons hold good with regard to Japan, and both the EEC and Japan are far less favoured with regard to material resources as a whole than North America. These features are reflected in the forecasts and show the expectation of relatively low rates of growth for the EEC with the US growing about ½% per annum faster. Japan is forecast to grow at 1% per annum faster than the US but this would still represent a near halving of that country's rate of growth up to 1973.

For the purposes of analysing the future economic power structure in relation to the role of the dollar, Canada should perhaps be included with the US. Thus in 1975 the US and Canada together accounted for more than 26% of world output compared with 24% for the EEC and less than 10% for Japan. Taking the forecast range of growth rates through the 1980s the US and Canadian share would have dropped to nearly 25% and the Japanese share risen to over 11%. By contrast the share of the EEC[2] would have dropped to less than 21%. Taking the projections through the 1990s the range of output growth forecasts would then result in the US and Canada having a share of world output of nearly 24% compared with less than 19% for the EEC and nearly 12% for Japan.

Thus, on those assumptions US output would still account for more than 20% of the world's total at the year 2000, but this would represent nearly 36% of the output of the OECD as a whole. When Canada is included with the US the share would amount to nearly 42%. The relative changes between the groups are reflected in *Chart 7.2*.

[2]No allowance has been made for future changes in membership beyond the nine at the time of writing in compiling estimates of future output levels of the EEC.

The countries outside the OECD are expected to grow at a faster rate, their share of world output increasing from 39% in 1975 to nearly 43% at the end of the century. This group includes the USSR and the East European communist countries as well as China and India, where output growth is forecast to improve significantly in both the 1980s and 1990s.

Taking the boundaries of the forecasts illustrated in *Chart 7.2,* the highest rate of growth forecast for the EEC would take its share of output to nearly 22% of the world's total by the year 2000, whereas the lowest end of the range of growth forecasts for the US and Canada would result in a share of just over 20%. Such a combination seems extremely unlikely and it must remain fairly certain that the US and Canada will still be the world's dominant economic group at the end of the century.

Moreover, the chances of the EEC challenging North America for leadership within this time seem slight, since the progress of its institutions towards an effective economic union has been extremely slow. Although the EEC will be enlarged by the inclusion of new members, it is not beyond the bounds of possibility that the UK may leave the EEC because of failure to agree on matters such as the Common Agricultural Policy and her contribution to the Community budget. Aspects of the development of a common European currency are discussed in the following chapter.

The continued dominance of the US in world trade and commerce

The profile of output growth outlined in the preceding section suggests that it is exceedingly unlikely that the US will have lost its dominant position within the world economy before the year 2000. Indeed, the evidence indicates that the only possibility of the US being overtaken in this period lies in a more buoyant performance on the part of a unified EEC. We put odds against this eventuality and it seems more probable that the US and Canada will remain the world's largest output unit until well on in the twentyfirst century.

In this connection it is perhaps helpful to contrast this scenario of the future world power structure with the overtaking and eclipse of the UK by the US over the past hundred years. It was roughly a century ago, in the 1880s, that the US overtook the UK in terms of shares of world industrial production. The continued expansion of the US into leadership from that point was aided by a much faster growth in population than the UK and her neighbouring European countries. It was also the case that compared to the US, the European economies suffered relative setbacks of some magnitude in both the world wars of the twentieth century.

By contrast, neither Japan nor the EEC has the advantage of faster population growth over the next 20 years to help overtake the US in terms of total output. The reverse is the case with the EEC so that for the EEC bloc to overtake the US it is necessary to postulate a major setback to output growth in the US, as might be brought about by involvement in a world war while the Common Market bloc remained neutral in such a conflict, suffering far less in terms of economic disruption. Although possible, such a prospect seems highly unlikely.

Another possibility of the US losing its dominant position could arise if the attempts to curb price inflation failed so that inflation there rose above, and stayed significantly above, the average of competing countries for a protracted period. It is probable that higher inflation rates would result in lower output growth. If, at the same time, the US inflation rate exceeded the average of the industrialized countries, confidence in the dollar would be eroded and other alternatives would be sought in preference to the dollar as a reserve asset. Even so, the process would more likely to be gradual than sudden and in any event we have already placed low odds on a relative worsening of the US performance in terms of the relative rate of price inflation.

Doubts have been expressed at the capacity of the US economy to expand at more than a modest pace in the future because of the decline in her rate of growth in labour productivity. This in turn reflects the low rate of ploughback of national income into investment compared with Japan and the EEC. Moreover, the proportion of personal income saved has been extremely low in recent years, suggesting that the US economy is tending towards stagnation and that recovery from the 1980–1981 recession will be modest.

The argument is valid, but only if it is assumed the US now lacks those dynamic qualities needed to respond to difficulties and to generate the investment needed to exploit new technology in the fields of energy, electronics, biochemistry and defence which offer strong opportunities for expansion in the 1980s and 1990s. We argue, however, that the awareness of the problem of low investment and productivity growth will result in government policies designed to stimulate productive investment and that US business is well capable of responding to such a stimulus. Moreover, with a decline in the rate of price inflation, the prospects for expansion of productive investment would tend to be enhanced.

For these reasons, we conclude that although US output growth will be less in the 1980s and 1990s than in the 1950s and 1960s, it will not be inferior to the average rate of growth of the EEC group of countries and will probably exceed that average to some extent by virtue of the superior US position *vis à vis* energy resources. Thus the dominant position of the US in world output is unlikely to be eroded by more than a modest extent through the rest of this century.

Neither is it likely that the dominance of the US economy in terms of output will be accompanied by a significant decline in the American share of world trade and commerce. In making comparisons it must be remembered that within the EEC there is an extremely large element of trade between the members. If these transactions are excluded, then the Common Market's external trade with the rest of the world assumes a smaller proportion. Even without such an adjustment the US accounts for roughly 14% of total world merchandise trade taking both exports and imports. When the foreign transactions of the US in services and invisibles are taken into the reckoning, then her share of world trade on this basis increases to almost 18%. And when the double counting of inter-Common Market trade is stripped from the figures, the US share of world trade in goods and services is not far short of 23%.

We conclude, therefore, that the domestic share of the US and Canada in world trade as a whole will not be overtaken by the EEC bloc nor by Japan in this century. It seems highly improbable that the US will undergo any relative decline comparable to that of the UK from its peak in 1870. It should also be borne in mind that sterling continued as the world's major reserve currency and common unit of account up to the First World War, and that its position as a reserve currency was only overhauled by the US dollar in the inter-war period. Even allowing for an acceleration in the pace of change through the past century, the world's smaller economic power units are unlikely to overtake the US in terms of output and trade for a long time to come and almost certainly not in the twentieth century.

Against that background we now turn to consider alternative currency units to the US dollar and likely developments within the EEC and the IMF system.

8
Composite reserve units

Special drawing rights

With the price of gold fixed at its 1934 valuation, there was growing concern during the 1960s at the fast growth in world trade in relation to official reserves of gold and foreign currency. One solution—and the neatest—would have been to raise the price of gold. However, the argument against an increase in the gold price proved paramount and attention was forced towards alternative means of raising international reserve facilities.

The political argument against raising the gold price had widespread support. South Africa and Russia, as the world's largest gold producers, stood to gain in substantial measure from a price increase. Objections to the nature of the political regimes in those two countries were reflected in opposition to a revision of the price. With hindsight, an increase in the price of gold at that stage to reflect the depreciation in the value of money over the previous 30 years *might* have staved off the turmoils of the 1970s, and it is of interest to note that the free market price of gold rose to such a point in 1980 as to more than compensate for the rise in domestic prices in the US since 1934. Moreover, the gains to South Africa and the USSR from the price escalation were vast compared with the kind of gold price increase mooted in the 1960s. Even so, the argument in South Africa's case is double-sided for the balance of payments contribution from gold sales at enhanced prices tends towards an overvalued exchange rate on purchasing power considerations and thus increases the country's dependence on imports of manufactures and depresses non-gold exports.

In view of the opposition to an increase in the price of gold, discussions were initiated into the possibility of introducing a new form of reserve asset. A study group was set up under the aegis of the Group of Ten and the question of the 'adjustment' process was referred to a working party of the Economic Policy Committee of the OECD. The study group, under the chairmanship of S. Ossola, reported in 1965, outlining the problems rather than producing an agreed recommendation. One of the fears at that time was that open discussion of reform would further undermine confidence and increase speculative movements of funds. It was also argued that the real problem was one of imbalance between the major economies and currencies and that reform in the shape of new international credit facilities or new reserve assets would simply delay the adoption of the necessary economic policies to overcome the fundamental disequilibrium. In other words, the US would be able to put off setting her own house in order.

However, in 1967, following meetings between the Deputies of the Group of Ten and the Executive Directors of the IMF, an agreed scheme was presented to the annual meeting of the Fund at Rio de Janeiro. Following agreement in principle, the scheme was agreed in detail in March 1968 and approved by the IMF governors in May. This provided for the creation of Special Drawing Rights (SDRs), as distinct from the ordinary drawing rights of the Fund's members.

The scheme provided that, at the beginning of each period, each member would have its account credited with its share of the total amount of SDRs to be created. The 'rationing' of the issues was to be proportionate to existing Fund quotas. The SDR was to be equivalent to one US dollar's worth of gold and was to be available for use in settling imbalances in payments. A member could in these circumstances buy currencies with SDRs and other members would be obliged to accept the new reserve units in exchange for their currencies, and to hold them up to an amount equal to three times the member's own cumulative allocation[1].

Decisions with respect to the issue of SDRs were to be made by an 85% weighted vote of the governors of the Fund on the basis of five-year projections of the need for international liquidity as proposed by the Managing Director of the Fund. Although technically the new units were to be drawing rights and not reserve assets, this was a matter of form only for they were to be freely usable, subject only to the restriction that each country must hold an average of 30% of its allocation during any five-year period.

The scheme was ratified during 1968 and 1969 and the first issue of SDRs was made on 1st January 1970 amounting to 3414 million units. This was followed by further issues of 2949 million units a year later, and 2952 million units on 1st January 1972. The units were linked to gold and were given a value equal to 0.888671 grams of fine gold, a valuation which subsequently had little relevance in view of the breaking of the dollar link with gold and the attempt to demonetize gold. The key relationship was directly with currencies and the SDR was a composite unit make up of a basket of currencies, which was later amended as shown in *Table 8.1*.

Whereas the ordinary drawing right system enables members to draw on those deposits made to the Fund and to receive credits from the Fund, there is no common fund under the SDR system from which members can draw to acquire foreign exchange. The SDR belongs to the member and enables him to 'draw' on other countries, acquiring foreign exchange in return for the SDR.

The SDRs may be transferred directly from one country to another without direction or designation from the IMF for repurchase of the national currency. This facility has been found convenient for the settlement of support operations in the exchange markets.

In the case of an indirect transaction, SDRs are transferred by one country to another in return for foreign currency. The receiving country is, however, designated by the IMF and given foreign currency in exchange for the SDRs.

[1]HIRSCH, F. (1969). *Money International*, pp.584–585. Harmondsworth; Penguin.

Table 8.1 Composition of the SDR basket from 1 July 1974[2]

	%
US dollar	33.0
Deutschemark	12.5
Sterling	9.0
French franc	7.5
Japanese yen	7.5
Canadian dollar	6.0
Italian lira	6.0
Netherlands guilder	4.5
Belgian franc	3.5
Swedish krona	2.5
Australian dollar	1.5
Danish krone	1.5
Norwegian krone	1.5
Spanish peseta	1.5
Austrian schilling	1.0
South African rand	1.0
	100.0

This rests considerable powers with the Fund but is subject to certain rules. Firstly, the country nominated must be in a sufficiently strong economic position. Every effort must then be made to ensure a balanced spread of holdings of SDRs and priority must be given to certain transactions. Finally, no country may be obliged to accept more than twice its SDR quota.

In addition, the credit country may not offer just any foreign currency in exchange and the currencies offered must be freely convertible. This means that the country of issue may not impose restrictions with regard to current payments and may not discriminate against certain countries, nor may it introduce multiple rates of exchange. Subsequently it was specified that the US dollar, sterling, the French franc, the deutschemark, the Italian lira, the Mexican peso and the Netherlands guilder ranked as convertible.

Restrictions are also imposed on the use of SDRs. Although a country may have used up all its SDRs over a certain period and is thus not obliged to maintain a minimum amount of SDRs, it is still required to maintain an average amount of SDRs over a number of years. This 'reconstruction' obligation is comparable with the obligation to repay a credit. Therefore, over a period of five years, each country is obliged to maintain a daily average of SDRs not less than 30% of the average of the daily net cumulative allocations.

Countries which hold SDRs receive interest on the portion that is drawn on them, i.e. on the difference between the amount held and the amount allotted. Initially, the rate of interest was fixed at 1½%, a particularly low rate, which was insisted upon by the US for fear that the SDR would undermine the dollar as a reserve instrument. However, with the mounting scale of the US payments deficits, the glut of dollars available as international reserves escalated to embarrassing proportions, forcing the devaluation of the dollar and an increase

[2]How does the Special Drawing Rights System work (June 1975). *Kreditbank Weekly Bulletin No. 24*. Brussels.

in the gold price. This, in turn, necessitated the revaluation of the SDR. At the same time, the declining role of gold in international settlements and growing unwillingness to hold dollars enhanced the status and role of the SDR. This also entailed the raising of the rate of interest to reflect market rates, the SDR rates being fixed lower than market rates because of the inherent stability of the composite unit. The settlement of interest payments is undertaken by the IMF.

It is doubtful, however, whether it was a correct decision to fix the rate of interest on the SDR below market rates. Viewed as a reserve asset in competition with other reserve units in the shape of national currencies, a currency commanding confidence may be regarded equally as attractive, if not more so, than the SDR; and it can be argued that the rate of interest should be fixed not lower than the average of prevailing short-term interest rates of countries with strong currencies.

At the start, the developing countries, which received relatively few SDRs in the initial allocations, used the greater part of their allocations, currencies being supplied by the industrial countries. Among the latter the US, the UK, Italy and France were the largest users of the new facility; Germany, the Netherlands and Belgium were the main creditors.

It was, perhaps, ironical that the creation of SDRs to increase international liquidity occurred at a time when US payments deficits in the last phases of the Vietnam War reached record proportions, thus increasing world liquidity at the very same time. In fact, the world stood in need of a new reserve unit and a reduction of dollar liabilities. It was also the case that the loss of confidence in the dollar highlighted the need for a new reference point, or unit of value, for the world's exchange system. The Bretton Woods regime had rested upon gold as the common denominator for currency values. The values of the SDR and the dollar began to diverge from August 1971, when the US suspended gold convertibility, and widened further when the dollar was devalued in December of that year, and again in February 1973. Fortuitously, a new international unit, or *numéraire*, was at hand in the shape of the SDR and in this sense the role of the IMF has tended to increase in importance.

The distribution of SDRs has been increased from 1979 and the pattern of holdings is shown in *Table 8.2*. Similarly, the composition of the SDR basket has changed, as shown in *Table 8.3*, having been modified to include the major oil exporters.

The central rates of the parities of the 'basket' currencies making up the SDR serve to determine its value and this, in turn, serves as a reference point for the value of individual currencies. Indeed, many countries began to express the central rate of their currencies in terms of the SDR. As a unit of account, therefore, the SDR fills an important need in the international reserve system. Since it is the commodity characteristic of gold which determines its price rather than international agreement between central banks, it is inferior to the SDR as a unit of account, although perhaps still more important as a reserve asset.

Another important feature of the SDR is its use in both increasing and distributing world liquidity. Apart from supplementing foreign currencies and gold as reserve assets, a means exists for discrimination in the distribution of reserve increases. It would be possible, for example, to make SDR distributions solely to poor countries, thus increasing their purchasing power in international trade. This would represent an indirect granting of aid from

Table 8.2 SDR holdings as at January 1980

	SDR (billion)	*Percentage of total*
United States	2.94	18.1
West Germany	1.81	11.1
Japan	1.46	9.0
United Kingdom	1.10	6.8
France	0.86	5.3
Canada	0.59	3.6
Italy	0.59	3.6
Belgium	0.57	3.5
India	0.50	3.1
Netherlands	0.50	3.1
Brazil	0.37	2.2
Venezuela	0.34	2.1
Argentina	0.30	1.9
Spain	0.27	1.6
Iran	0.24	1.5
Others	3.82	23.5
Total	16.25	100.0

Source: *The Economist,* March 22, 1980

richer to poorer countries. Such a procedure would, however, depart from the strictly monetary role of a unit of account and a reserve asset and would become the subject of political considerations of far reaching consequences, discussed in the final chapter.

Finally, although the SDR has proved a workable composite reserve currency unit, it must be recognized that it offers no more than a partial solution to

Table 8.3 SDR basket as at February 1980

	Units of currency included	*Percentage weight in basket*
US dollar	0.40	30.6
Deutschemark	0.32	13.9
Sterling	0.05	8.7
French franc	0.42	7.8
Japanese yen	21.00	6.5
Netherlands guilder	0.14	5.5
Italian lira	52.00	4.9
Canadian dollar	0.07	4.7
Belgian franc	1.60	4.3
Saudi riyal	0.13	3.0
Swedish krone	0.11	2.0
Iranian rial	1.70	1.8
Spanish peseta	1.50	1.7
Austrian schilling	0.28	1.7
Norwegian krone	0.10	1.5
Australian dollar	0.017	1.4
		100.0

Source: *The Economist,* March 22, 1980

the problem of 'dollar indigestion'. A wholesale switch out of unwanted dollars into SDRs is out of the question for the obvious reason that the SDR itself contains such a large dollar component. It is this feature which inhibits its use as a means of exchange for in commercial transactions the users of currencies need to finish up with specific currencies with which to settle. The complexity of having to 'unscramble' something like an SDR to buy machinery in Germany, for example, illustrates one of the main limitations of the composite currency unit[3]. This particular feature will be equally true in the establishment of a composite European currency unit.

The European monetary system

On the breakdown of the fixed exchange rate system a group of European countries endeavoured to maintain a degree of stability in their exchange operations by collaborating to restrict exchange rate fluctuations between their currencies through active intervention. The joint float—the 'snake'—obliged the participants to limit their exchange rate movements to specific agreed limits, or bands, against the US dollar. There was a strong motive for members of the EEC to adopt such a scheme since the Common Agricultural Policy (CAP), which could be regarded as the cornerstone of the EEC, entailed complex transactions between members and a composite unit of account based on the US dollar, the 'green' currency system in use for pricing agricultural products and farm settlements within the Community. It was also the view that the parity system used to operate the CAP would prepare the way for the ultimate introduction of a European Monetary Union with a common currency.

From April 1972, therefore, the EEC members reduced the permitted range of fluctuation of their currencies to 2¼%. At the same time, the snake as a whole was permitted to move within a wider margin of 4½% against the dollar, giving rise to the graphic and colourful term 'snake in the tunnel'. However, the breakdown of the fixed parity arrangements under the Smithsonian Agreement and the US devaluation of February 1973 led to a general regime of floating exchange rates. The 'snake' members decided to float their currencies jointly against all other currencies whilst maintaining the 2¼% band between their respective currencies. This was the basis of the revised joint float, or 'snake in a lake'. Other European countries joined members of the EEC in the joint float, though not all EEC members participated. By implication, membership of the joint float required harmonization of domestic economic policies and in this sense the arrangement was restrictive; the tendency was for other members to be tied to Germany, the strongest economy with the strongest currency, and for monetary policy to be dictated to some extent by German monetary policy.

The operation of the joint float provided useful experience in harmonization of policies and exchange management and, after discussions and negotiations during 1978, agreement was reached between heads of EEC member governments in December of that year to introduce a new system—the European Monetary System (EMS). The scheme began to operate in March 1979. The UK decided not to join at the outset, and Italy and Eire became members with special concessions.

[3]The SDR composition has been further changed—see p.133.

There are three main components of the EMS. These are an exchange rate mechanism, the European Monetary Fund (EMF) and the credit facilities. These elements are linked by the European Currency Unit (ECU), which is the same as the European Unit of Account (EUA), namely a basket of currencies composed of the weighted average of member currencies, similar in substance to the SDR. The ECU is intended to be a new reserve asset for use as the eventual settlement base of the system and in the determination of intervention limits for member currencies. The members' central banks were to receive an initial supply of ECUs by depositing 20% of their existing gold and dollar reserves into a joint pool and the intention was that by 1981 the pool of reserves would be used to form the basis of the EMF. The Fund would then police the system and co-ordinate further integration.

In the transitional phase members receive ECUs in exchange for the reserves deposited with the European Fund for Monetary Co-operation (EFMC) rolled over through exchanges at three-monthly intervals. The ECUs obtained through these exchanges are intended to be used mainly for equalizing balances between central banks, and although not a member of the exchange rate part of the scheme, the UK participated by making sterling part of the ECU and expressed its intention to maintain a 'stable' exchange rate. It also decided to keep its options open with regard to full membership at a later date.

Table 8.4 ECU weights at 13 March 1979

	%
Deutschemark	33.0
French franc	19.8
Sterling	13.4
Italian lira	9.5
Netherlands guilder	10.5
Belgian franc	9.2
Danish krone	3.1
Irish punt	1.2
Luxembourg franc	0.4
	100.0

The initial composition of the ECU is shown in *Table 8.4*. The weight of each currency is to be monitored and adjusted where necessary. In practice, the fixed number of units of each national currency within the basket results in fluctuating weights when these fixed units are valued at the exchange rates of the day.

With regard to the exchange rate system, Austria and Switzerland decided to maintain their tacit currency links with the deutschemark and were thus informally linked to the complicated EMS. The currency bloc is, therefore, considerably wider than under the old joint float and its mechanics are more rigorous.

The permitted margin of currency fluctuations was kept at 2¼% either side of a central parity, giving a maximum potential swing of 4½%. Because of their high inflation rates and weaker economic positions, Italy and Eire were permitted an initial band of fluctuation of 6% either side of parity, a concession taken up by Italy though not by Eire, despite her close economic ties with the UK.

The points at which central bank intervention is required to maintain a national currency within bounds is indicated by reference to a currency grid of parities. A new feature in the intervention mechanics is the 'ECU related divergence indicator'. The movement of a currency against the ECU basket provides an indication of the timing of official intervention in the exchange markets. The divergence indicator is calculated by reference to a formula reflecting the weight of the individual currency within the ECU and, with the exception of Italy, the formula is as follows:

Divergence indicator formula

$$\tfrac{3}{4} \times 2\tfrac{1}{4}\,(1 - \text{weight of currency in basket})\%$$

What this means is that the larger the weight of the currency (e.g. the deutschemark), the smaller the permitted fluctuation. The whole effect of the scheme, therefore, is to limit the degree of fluctuation to something considerably less than 2¼% either side of parity and closer to the intervention bands laid down under the original Bretton Woods system.

In practice, the deutschemark has been the benchmark for the system and other currencies have been forced towards alignment. In the first year of operation the Danish krone was devalued and the deutschemark revalued upwards by 2%. Sterling, being relatively strong, led to a revaluation of the pound against the ECU and the average change in parity of members' currencies was no more than 1.9% in contrast to an average swing of 5.2% in the six preceding years.

Greater stability in exchange rates within Europe has certainly contributed to an easing of the world problem so far as rates are concerned, although it has done little to ease the imbalance between the dollar and the rest of the world. Moreover, with regard to the world reserve system little contribution is to be expected from the new European system until the composite currency unit becomes part of an effective European Fund backed by a common currency. Progress in such a direction will inevitably be slow and will hinge upon a satisfactory outcome of a reform of the CAP and a much closer integration of the EEC national economies. Indeed, economic nationalism remains such a potent force within the Community that it seems unlikely that an effective European economic union will materialize. It is not beyond the bounds of possibility that a failure to adjust the UK's net contribution to the EEC budget to a more equitable basis will result in her leaving the Community, although in such an event an economic union between the remaining members might be less difficult to achieve. At the same time, it will be recognized that the broadening of the Community by the admission of new members, such as Greece and Portugal, would add to the difficulties in reaching an economic union equivalent in operation to the US.

With regard to the credit facilities available under the EMS, the central bank exchange arrangements were limited initially to 14 billion ECUs, providing short-term credit facilities for up to nine months. Medium-term credit was to be made available to all EEC members with an initial limit set at 11 billion ECUs. The total of these facilities amounted to the equivalent of around $34 billion, not a particularly large sum when compared with the balance of payments surpluses of the OPEC countries following the 1979–1980 oil price rises of around $100 billion per annum. Additional loan facilities were planned for weaker economies, such as Italy and Eire, to enable them to improve their economic potential. Five-year loans of up to one billion ECUs were to be made available at a rate of interest carrying a 3% subsidy. Only fully participating members in the EMS (i.e. not the UK) were to be eligible.

More than anything else the EMS represents a currency bloc, heavily influenced by the deutschemark. Since Germany has the lowest historical and potential rate of price inflation in the EEC, its relatively successful policies will, therefore, tend to influence her neighbours and contribute to a general lowering of the rate of price inflation. Such a contribution on the side of stability should be particularly welcome. Present evidence suggests, however, that the ECU is a long way from becoming a world reserve unit and the mechanism does not exist for ECUs to feature as reserve assets outside Europe.

The original plan envisaged phased progress towards a unified EEC economy with a central bank controlling monetary policy for the Community as a whole. The timetable anticipated the formation of a European Monetary Fund in 1981. It was also intended that the reserve funds provided by members (20% of national gold and dollar reserves) in the form of short-term exchanges for ECUs should be permanently pooled and doubled and placed under the management of the new Fund. From that point steps would be taken to issue the ECU as a reserve asset. The effect of this would be to increase European liquidity and, in view of the potential inflationary consequences of such a move, some member countries will undoubtedly resist the proposed changes. In other words, the timetable will not be met.

In the meantime, the EEC Commission and the Council will prepare plans for the second stage in conjunction with the governors of the members' central banks and the monetary committee. Whether or not such proposals will be adopted will depend, as always in the EEC, on the lowest common denominator of political acceptability of the national governments. Compromises have to be made to achieve agreement between heads of governments and this generally results in delay and slower progress than originally envisaged.

Mr Jacques van Ypersele, the chairman of the monetary committee responsible for formulating the first stage of the EMS, outlined the following programme for a second stage.

(1) 20% of member countries' dollar reserves would be permanently transferred to the EMF as well as national currencies of an equal value. Gold would only be loaned, or exhcnaged, as at present.
(2) Each member would receive ECUs in return. Those issued in exchange for gold and dollars could be used freely, while those issued in exchange for national currencies would be 'blocked'. The latter would only be available for short or medium-term loans to members.
(3) ECUs would rank as a currency convertible into other currencies.
(4) Members' central banks would continue to be responsible for intervening to support their own currencies, but the foreign exchange needed would come from the EMF.
(5) The EMF would be run by the governors of the members' central banks and they would decide on exchange rate variations and on conditions for loans made in blocked ECUs.
(6) A target zone for the EMS currencies (presumably the ECU) against the

dollar would be determined so as to pave the way for co-ordination between Europe and the US.

While the expansion of the Fund and the organization of loan facilities seem politically acceptable, and therefore attainable in the short-run, the target of a convertible ECU, implying a European currency and a European monetary policy, is unlikely to be achieved in a second stage of development. The attainment of such a goal seems unlikely until the CAP has been radically overhauled and the EEC budgetary system reformed into a stable system. Most importantly, progress towards this form of European union is likely to be modest until such time as the EEC members harmonize their political and economic objectives to such as extent as to coincide with national self-interests. Comparing the position today with that in 1957, when the Community came into being, some progress has been made in subordinating nationalist pressures and interests within the Community. Based on the rate of progress to date, however, full monetary union, under which a unified European currency ranking as a world reserve unit would be established, seems unlikely to reach fruition before 1990.

The community of interest may well strengthen during the 1980s if the system of intervention in the exchange markets continues to smooth the European parities in such a way as to help trade within the Community as well as to contribute to a slowing down in the rate of price inflation. If the disparities in the rate of price inflation between members are narrowed sufficiently in this process, the objections to sacrificing national economic sovereignty to a European Community sovereignty would be whittled away.

It will be apparent that the proposals for the development of a European Monetary Fund imply a reduction in the influence of the IMF for the European members; the new facilities would supplement the facilities available from the IMF. In a sense this might release IMF resources for use in other areas, although this would be by no means certain for the IMF's role and influence could be diminished. The value of the world system of a fully-fledged European currency and reserve asset would lie in the potential reduction of the role of the dollar and an easing of the burden on the US that the prime reserve role imposes on the country. It is the case, therefore, that the successful evolution of a European monetary system could contribute towards a solution of the world exchange and reserve problem.

The substitution account

Apart from the possibility of the development of the EMU as a composite currency to rank with the dollar as a reserve asset, a scheme has been mooted to expand the role of the SDR, substituting SDRs for dollars. The proposal, under discussion at the IMF, would allow central banks to exchange part of their dollar holdings for Fund issued assets denominated in SDRs. There is some concern at the tendency for central banks to diversify their reserves away from the dollar and towards a multi-currency reserve system and it is argued that this may prove inherently unstable as shifts in central banks' currency preferences could disrupt the foreign exchange markets.

In preference, it is argued that a substitution account would help to promote the use of the SDR as a reserve asset and offer an alternative means of diversification out of the dollar, but in an orderly fashion, thus reducing the dollar's reserve role. The scale of such a move is envisaged at some SDR 50 billion (equivalent to $65 billion) although the IMF contemplates an initial issue of around $20 billion—a particularly small amount compared with the current OPEC surplus of around $100 billion a year. The argument in favour of some scheme of reserve diversification rests on the fact that some 80% of the world's foreign exchange reserves are presently held in dollars. In fact, reserves have been diversified out of sterling into hard currencies such as the deutschemark during the 1970s and smaller industrialized countries have moved out of the dollar. But the larger European countries and Japan have accumulated dollars as a result of a support operation for the dollar and this has maintained the overall dependence on the dollar as a reserve asset.

Nevertheless, diversification is expected to continue and increase, aided of course by the operation of the multinational banks in the Eurocurrency market. This then is the case for the introduction of the substitution account and it is further argued that the surpluses of the oil-exporting countries make the problem more urgent. It is suggested the scheme should be voluntary, although wide participation would be essential for its success. To add to its attractions, the scheme would require a more realistic rate of interest on SDRs with interest paid on a weighted average of short-term rates ruling in the major financial markets. Such a change is necessary in any case to enhance the attraction of the present SDR system.

A further innovation is the suggestion that claims should be freely transferable between official and private holders by mutual agreement and that the inclusion of the private sector in the account would enhance the liquidity of the claims and pave the way for the eventual private use of the SDRs proper, though private holders of dollars would not be permitted in the initial stages to deposit those dollars with the account. These proposals have the backing of a New York based study group of bankers and economists supported by the Rockefeller Foundation under the label of the 'Group of 30'.

There are strong objections to the proposed substitution account scheme, partly because of its technical complexity. The main objection is that the IMF would be at considerable risk in acquiring the large volume of dollars, to be invested in US Treasury securities, in exchange for a liability denominated in SDRs. To cover the exchange risk it has been suggested that the IMF should use its gold holdings and, in view of the popularity of gold as a reserve asset, there may well be a general unwillingness on the part of the IMF members to support the proposal.

It is also the case that the policies of the US aimed at reducing price inflation and the effects of the 1980–1981 recession will both improve the US balance of payments and enhance the attractions of the dollar. This in turn would tend to weaken support within the US for the substitution account proposals, although a phase in which the US dollar was strengthening would be an ideal occasion for launching the scheme. There would be no stampede out of dollars and the transition could take place in an orderly way.

Other practical objections are likely to be raised by other countries. Germany, for example, in balance of payments deficit as a result of the sharp rise in the oil import bill, has an interest in issuing long-term deutschemark loans, thus encouraging reserve diversifications into marks. The wider use of SDRs as reserve assets would to some degree run counter to the greater reserve role of the deutschemark.

Perhaps of greater importance, large dollar reserve holders in the Third World—the main diversifiers in recent years—are worried that the SDR substitution account would serve to withdraw funds from the Eurocurrency market and add to the difficulty of borrowing in support of payment deficits and expansion plans.

There are also obstacles in the way of implementation of the scheme since the substitution account would require legislation in most countries. Ratification would be a lengthy process; moreover, general acceptance may prove to be unattainable. The debate has been further complicated by the Brandt commission's report advocating the issue of SDRs as a form of aid to poorer, developing countries which would in effect represent a transfer of purchasing power from the rich to the poor. The prospective recipients of aid are unlikely to support the substitution proposals since the scheme would probably block the adoption of the Brandt proposals, which in turn appear to have scant prospects of being adopted because of objections by the richer countries.

We are forced to the conclusion, therefore, that the reduction of the reserve role of the dollar is unlikely to be achieved by the wider use of composite units of account for the expansion of the role of the SDR will probably be restricted[4] and the development of the EMS will be slow and unlikely for many years to produce a unified European currency to rank as a world reserve asset. If there is to be an alternative to the dollar it seems more probable that other currencies will feature to a greater extent in the reserve role. More to the point, the failure of the attempt to move towards the demonetization of gold means that the world still has a universally accepted reserve asset at hand. The strongly enhanced price of gold also means that the significance of gold in official reserve assets has increased, and to such an extent that the role of gold must be reconsidered in that it could offer a practical solution to the world's reserve and exchange system. This possibility is considered and discussed in the following chapter.

[4]Since this chapter was written, there has been a further change in the composition of the SDR, discussed in a postscript (p.133).

9

The future world reserve system

Exchange reserves are currently held in five main categories. These are:

(1) gold
(2) IMF accounts
(3) SDRs
(4) US dollars
(5) other reserve currencies

The gold element in reserves is subject to fluctuations in value in the absence of a fixed price and different countries adopt different formulae for determining a price at which to value their holdings. The valuations tend to be significantly below the open market price, a prudent practice in view of the extreme price movements.

The IMF gives the following estimates of world reserves with gold holdings valued at SDR35 per ounce. The valuations in *Table 9.1* are expressed in SDRs.

Table 9.1 World reserves as at the end of 1979

	*Billions of SDRs**
Reserve positions in IMF	11.8
SDRs	12.5
Foreign exchange	246.1
Gold	32.5
Total	302.9

*1 SDR = $1.31733
Source: *IMF International Financial Statistics Yearbook*

If the gold holdings are valued at $400 per ounce, world official gold holdings are increased by SDR250 billion to SDR282 billion and total world reserves are increased by 83% to SDR553 billion.

On that valuation, the distribution of world reserves is shown in *Table 9.2*. The estimate must be regarded as an approximation since the volume of gold holdings will have changed to a small extent as a result of gold sales by the IMF and the US since that date. It is also the case that the gold holdings of the reserve positions in the IMF are understated. However, the main feature of the make-up of reserves is the dominant position of gold when valued at something approaching the market price and the insignificant position of SDRs and reserve positions in the IMF.

Table 9.2 World reserves including gold revaluation

	%
Reserve positions in IMF	2.1
SDRs	2.3
Foreign exchange	44.6
Gold at $400 per ounce	51.0
Total	100.0

The importance of gold in relation to dollar holdings is particularly important, for at a price of SDR35 per ounce, gold accounted for only 11% of world reserves while dollars accounted for 65%. The dominant position of the dollar as a world reserve asset was therefore extreme. Indeed, if the dollar element of the IMF holdings and SDRs is added to dollar foreign exchange reserve holdings, the dependence on the dollar is seen to be even greater. But with gold valued at $400 per ounce the relative position is transformed, dollars accounting for no more than 35% of world reserves, including the IMF and SDR dollar components, while gold accounts for over half of world reserves.

It is against that background, and taking into account our analysis of the future world power structure, inflation, Eurocurrency market and composite currency units, that we now consider the possible developments in the world reserve system.

The need for a freely convertible unit of account

The present international system has evolved to meet the needs of world trade and commerce. Throughout history systems have seldom been imposed by governments at the international level with any degree of success. Indeed, government regulation of domestic currencies has been haphazard and clumsy. Rather, systems have evolved through the operation of market forces, and it is these forces which have tended to influence and guide the development of domestic monetary systems. The same is true in the international sphere and the creation of the IMF has been the only occasion on which an international system was imposed as a result of a worldwide international agreement.

There is a parallel between the needs of a domestic economy and the world economy with regard to the means of exchange. Domestically, the public requires a convenient and acceptable unit of account commanding complete confidence as a means of exchange both for daily transactions in small denominations, as well as facilitating large capital transactions. The common feature is, of course, a unit of account which will serve for transactions of any size. Thus, by the same token, world commerce requires an acceptable unit of account which is freely convertible from currency to currency.

In the still wider field, the world monetary system also requires an acceptable unit in which there is absolute confidence and which may be freely given and accepted as a means of settlement in all countries. Today that role is filled somewhat uneasily by the US dollar, supplemented by the modest use of other currencies such as the deutschemark, sterling, the yen and the Swiss franc, as well as the SDR for official transactions. The great bulk of transactions is conducted between commercial banks on behalf of private commerce. Their requirements are almost entirely met through the exchange of national currencies, and composite units such as the SDR and EMU do not feature to any extent in commercial transactions. Neither is gold used in this capacity. Use of gold and composite units is virtually restricted to official settlements and the usefulness of these instruments as part of a world reserve system is dependent upon there being adequate links between reserve currencies and other instruments suitable for large official settlements.

For practical purposes, therefore, the world's requirement is for an acceptable and freely convertible unit of account which almost certainly has to be one or more of the leading national currencies.

Recycling of funds and the Brandt Report

The perpetual changes in balance of payments between countries lead to continuous changes in each country's reserves in one form or another. Throughout the 1970s the comparative size of the imbalances increased dramatically, first as a result of the huge US payments deficits, and then because of the violent adjustments in the world price of oil. With the continued shortage of oil in the 1980s, further increases in oil prices will tend to maintain wide imbalances in payments between countries. Some of the oil-exporting countries will continue to accumulate large liquid balances, while countries deficient in oil tend to experience payments deficits which will in some cases prove increasingly embarrassing.

The need for the recycling of funds between countries on a large scale will be a continuing feature of the next decade and possibly longer. In the 1990s, for example, industrial materials other than oil may move into persistent shortage resulting in price rises embarrassing to the importing country and generating payments surpluses for large exporters of the scarce materials.

Another aspect of the need for the recycling of funds has been highlighted by the Brandt Commission's report 'North—South'. That report drew attention to the widening gap between the richer and poorer countries, which lie broadly in the North or the South respectively, and the need for an increasing flow of development funds to help the expansion of the poorer countries of the South. The report argues that the self-interest of the northern countries requires that they should assist the poorer countries since trade with the South generates business and employment in the richer countries of the North.

Amongst the changes proposed by the Brandt report is the reform of the IMF, enabling that body to create additional liquidity for the benefit of the poorer countries. The need to recycle funds to put them at work where they are most needed in terms of world development is seen to be of crucial importance and the report is to be welcomed in drawing attention to the urgency of the world's problems and needs.

However, political programmes to achieve the recycling of funds in this way are notoriously difficult to bring to fruition because of the problem of securing agreement between large numbers of countries having diverse national self-interests. Little is to be looked for in progress along these lines in the short-run, and the world will continue to depend upon the successful operations of the Eurocurrency markets for the transfer of the large surplus funds of the oil-exporting countries to those countries needing to employ the foreign capital. But since the commercial international capital market cannot be expected to shoulder the risks of investing in countries with a low degree of credit-worthiness, it will be necessary to strengthen the role of official international institutions such as the IMF and World Bank. It must be recognized, however, that the Eurocurrency markets are indispensable for the relatively smooth recycling of funds around the world and that the IMF cannot be expanded in a short space of time to take over the role of the wider international capital market.

The IMF system and the SDR

Progress in reforming the IMF system has been slow and protracted. As we have seen, the use of IMF facilities by way of drawing rights and credits has been on a modest scale and in recent years the Eurocurrency markets have provided a greater source of funds to deficit countries than the IMF. In addition, the attempt to create an expansion of world liquidity and reserve facilities by means of SDR has not been particularly successful. SDRs account for little more than 2% of world reserves and their complexity has proved an obstacle to their widespread adoption as an international means of settlement. There is a current proposal to revise the SDR basket of currencies and to reconstruct the composition of the basket limiting it to, say, five major currencies[1]. This would add to the usefulness of the SDR as a means of exchange but the problems of securing international agreement through such a cumbersome organization as the IMF makes it extremely unlikely that the volume of SDRs will be expanded to the point where the unit becomes the world's major reserve asset.

The problem of reforming the IMF lies in its worldwide membership and democratic structure. The interests of members are extremely divergent and the inherent characteristic of the Fund as a lender of 'last resort', imposing strict terms on borrowing members, reduces its attractions to deficit countries. Moreover, the abandonment of the dollar link to gold and fixed exchange parities in the early 1970s served to undermine the basis of the Bretton Woods system, so that the IMF today has relatively little authority over the world's monetary system. It would require a return to gold and fixed parities to restore the authority of the IMF. Such a change is unlikely to come about under the aegis of the Fund and it is more probable that any change along these lines would be arrived at by the ad hoc decisions of the major powers.

Neither is there likely to be progress towards the adoption of the principle of a 'substitution account' whereby surplus dollars would be exchanged for SDRs. In the short-run, recession in the US is likely to strengthen her balance of payments and the return to surplus will probably strengthen the dollar and

[1]This reform was brought into effect from 1 January 1981.

encourage capital inflows into the US. Thus the problem of surplus dollars seems likely to diminish for the time being, unless the US becomes involved in war.

Excepting that possibility and looking further ahead, the gradual development in indigenous energy resources in the US will lessen her dependence on imported oil and contribute to a more permanent improvement in her balance of payments. In this connection, much will depend on the progress made in the US in reducing the rate of price inflation. We have argued that the adoption of stricter measures of credit control will limit the growth in money supply and lead to a reduction in the rate of inflation. It seems probable, therefore, that the US inflation rate will fall back to the average of the industrial countries in the short-run and then decline below the international average later in the 1980s. Thus the US dollar seems likely to improve in its relative attraction and the need for some special system of switching from the dollar into other reserve assets, such as the SDR, will probably diminish.

An additional factor is the enhanced value of gold as a world reserve asset at the high open-market price now established. If gold becomes a more active component of the world's reserve system then the importance of the dollar will be diminished, and the problem of excess dollars would also shrink in importance.

The European monetary system

Although we do not foresee the expansion of the SDR system as a likely solution to the world's exchange requirements, it must be recognized that the SDR has provided a useful unit of account as the *numéraire* of the world reserve system. Its usefulness in this respect, however, is limited since in commercial transactions national currencies perform the role of *numéraire* and the SDR is particularly unsuitable for that purpose.

The same objection will apply to the Common Market's development of the EMU. Whereas the composite unit will be of use in settling balances between member countries of the Common Market at the official level, it will not be suitable for commercial settlements. And again, it is extremely unlikely that the Common Market partners will reach agreement on the adoption of a common monetary system with a Common Market central bank operating a common currency throughout the EEC. With the enlargement of the Common Market membership, agreement will be still more difficult to obtain and it is notable that the economic nationalism of members such as France seems so strong that the abandonment of national economic sovereignty in favour of a Common Market economic sovereignty must be regarded as a remote possibility. We believe that the degree of unity necessary within the Common Market to establish a common currency is unlikely to be achieved much before the end of the century, if at all. Even then, the size of the EEC economy and its trade in relation to the rest of the world will not reach the dominant position to enable a Common Market currency to replace the US dollar as the most commonly used unit of account. Therefore the EMU is unlikely to feature in the future as a major factor in the world's reserve system.

Reserve currencies

The paramount position of the US dollar as the world's reserve asset and means of exchange has originated with the expansion of the US to be the leading world economic power. As with the UK and the pound sterling, the US dollar has become the convenient unit of account for a great proportion of the world's commercial transactions. This role must be expected to continue.

At the same time, there has been a gradual diversification of official reserves into other currencies. This movement, however, is on a relatively small scale and although deutschemarks, Swiss francs and sterling all feature as reserve assets in countries' foreign exchange reserve portfolios, this has been in spite of a reluctance of those countries to have their currencies used as reserves.

It is difficult to assert whether or not reserve currency status is an advantage or a liability. In the US there is resistance to the idea of diminishing the role of the dollar and supplanting it with other vehicles, such as the SDR. Whether this is for prestige reasons or commercial interest is difficult to prove. Certainly the banking community will tend to derive benefits from the use of the national currency as the world's premier means of exchange. This was very much the case so far as sterling and the City of London were concerned and the same considerations must apply with regard to the US banking network today. In the case of the UK the skills and contacts generated over many years, involving an international capital market in London, served to generate continuing world-wide business long after the relative economic decline of the country. Those skills facilitated the development of the Eurodollar market, based firmly in London, to the great commercial benefit of the British banking system. Similar arguments would apply in the case of the US with the use of the dollar. But the question arises whether *the interests of the banking community are synonymous with the interests of the economy as a whole.* One of the problems which can be identified from the history of the gold standard and the sterling system was the repercussion of the business cycle in other countries on the London credit scene. With other countries' reserves held in sterling, a payments problem and credit contraction in another centre would result in a drawing on funds in London. With the operation of the gold standard the loss of gold from London resulted in a contraction of the British credit base. On that evidence the operation of a reserve currency subjected the reserve country to worldwide pressures so that international considerations could often prove superior to the interests of the domestic economy.

In the post-war period the US had not suffered from the disadvantages experienced by the UK in managing a reserve currency. For most of the period the problems of adjustment have fallen on individual countries without undue repercussions on the US generated by a general running down of dollar balances; this had been because of the worldwide use of the dollar, particularly in the absence of a gold standard.

The US has not been forced into an automatic contraction of her credit and money supply arising from a loss of gold. This is a key difference when one compares the old sterling reserve system and the dollar reserve system of today. Nevertheless, the fears remain in smaller countries that the use of their currencies as reserve currencies could lead to constrictions on their domestic economies. This was certainly true in the case of the UK in the post-war period though the reason lay in the inadequacy of her reserves in relation to the scale of her liabilities. In the case of Germany and Switzerland, and possibly Japan, such problems are less likely to arise and, in view of the swing of the German and Japanese economies into balance of payments deficit, it is possible that the rest of the world will acquire greater quantities of German and Japanese currencies which would then feature in world reserve assets.

The main objection to reserve status on the part of smaller countries is the size of international capital movements in relation to their domestic economies. The danger is that the scale of movements of capital either in or out of a country would be so great in relation to the domestic money supply as to unhinge domestic economic policies.

For these reasons it seems highly improbable that currencies other than the dollar will expand significantly as world reserve assets. Some further diversification from the dollar is to be expected and the scale of such diversification will depend on confidence and relative rates of inflation. Should the US fail to curb its domestic price inflation sufficiently, then other currencies will gain in relative attraction, assuming that their underlying rates of inflation are less than those in the US. Our forecasts suggest that Germany and Switzerland, for example, will continue to generate lower rates of inflation in the 1980s and for this reason their currencies will continue to be attractive as international assets. Even so, we anticipate that the relative position of the US will not deteriorate with regard to inflation to the point where there are large scale withdrawals and movements into other currencies. The widening of the world's portfolio of reserve currency holdings is likely to be gradual and the greater use of currencies other than the dollar will still leave the dollar as the principal reserve unit by an extremely wide margin.

An important feature with regard to the development of the world currency status is the expansion of investment abroad. In the case first of the UK and then of the US, the expansion of overseas investment contributed a great deal to the worldwide use of the pound and the dollar. For other currencies to achieve anything like this international status, a considerable expansion of a country's foreign investment would be required. Although both Germany and Japan have begun to increase the scale of such investment, their international involvement in other economies is still minute compared with that of the US. This is another reason for looking for no more than a modest increase in the use of currencies other than the dollar as world reserve units.

We therefore anticipate a limited expansion in the use of the deutschemark, Swiss franc, sterling, yen and the French franc as reserve currencies, sterling still continuing as a reserve currency in spite of the tendency towards above-average inflation in Britain. Its new status as a petro-currency, and the leading position of London in the Eurocurrency markets, will serve to restore sterling as a reserve currency to some extent.

Return to a gold standard

In the 1980 US Presidential election campaign Ronald Reagan and his advisers raised the prospect of a return to gold as a means of eradicating inflation. What seems to be envisaged is the linking of the US currency supply to a part of the official US gold holding and a fixing of the dollar in terms of gold. Such a move would, presumably, through the US fixed price of gold, force the rest of the world back towards something like the original Bretton Woods system of fixed parities in relation to the stable gold price.

That such a proposition has become feasible is due to the upward movement in the price of gold and the enhancement of the value of official gold holdings. It also reflects the growing dissatisfaction with high rates of price inflation and with the volatile behaviour of the foreign exchange markets. There can be no doubting the general unpopularity of large fluctuations in exchange rates to businessmen engaged in international commerce. Good international trade relationships depend upon an ability to maintain stable price quotations and to keep the incidence of price changes to a minimum. With exchange rates fluctuating by as much as 10% in either direction within a single year, it is extremely difficult to conduct international trade without experiencing extreme volatility in profits. There is therefore a strong body of opinion in favour of a return to a more stable regime. It is hardly surprising, considering the turbulence of the world's markets since the 1960s, that with an acceleration of price inflation there should not have been some nostalgic longing for a return to the automatic regulator of the gold standard system. It is widely believed that the gold standard as it operated up to 1914 resulted in stable prices. Whether such a system could be translated into the 1980s is a different matter since the world's political and economic systems have changed almost out of recognition.

The principle of the gold standard was based on the free movement of gold into and out of a country. Since a country's currency was fixed in terms of gold, the business cycle led to inflows and outflows of gold. With an inflow of gold the credit base expanded and the expansion of bank credit and money supply led to increased spending and output. The tempo of upswing may well have generated rising prices, the expansion of imports and a balance of payments deficit. The deficit in turn may have led to an outflow of gold, a contraction of credit and money supply, and a recession tending to reduce prices, diminish imports and to restore the balance of payments.

However, the system did not operate automatically; it required intervention by the central bank through the control of credit. It was necessary to adjust interest rates as the means of influencing the demand for funds and the magnitude of the swings in the business cycles up to the Second World War suggests that the operators of the system were not particularly skilled nor successful. Whether such a system could operate successfully today must be open to doubt. For one thing it is unlikely that in the modern political environment such controls and restrictions would be accepted readily by the general public as the necessary discipline for securing price stability. Businesses by and large operate on credit and the banking system generates profits from lending. There is, therefore, a tendency for credit deflation to be resisted by the majority of the community, except in exceptional and temporary circumstances.

This does not, however, rule out the possibility of the reinstatement of gold as a means of official settlements between countries. Even so, there is virtually no possibility of a return to a full gold standard with a gold coinage established as legal tender. The whole history of the coinage shows that almost always a gold coin had far too high a unit value for convenient use in day to day transactions. When Britain suspended gold in the Napoleonic Wars and issued notes, these became so popular on account of their convenience that the general public expressed a strong preference for the continuation of currency notes when the gold standard returned after the war. The sovereign was, of course, in general circulation for the next hundred years, but the great majority of transactions were carried out in notes and other coinage. Indeed, when the UK again went off gold in the First World War, the withdrawal of gold coins as legal tender raised no objections.

Therefore, in today's conditions, with gold at a far higher price than in the past, there is no chance of its being adopted as legal tender; the single gold coin would have far too high a value. Yet there is a further problem in connection with gold in that the open market price fluctuates by wide margins from day to day. The private demand for gold has been substantial, fuelled by the dangerous acceleration in price inflation. There is an extremely wide attachment throughout the world's population to gold as a long-term store of value. For this reason political uncertainties and the threats of war result in sudden surges in demand for gold which are reflected in sharp increases in price in the open market. Conversely, when conditions stabilize to some extent and political uncertainties decrease, sharp rises in the price of gold tend to be reversed, as speculators take profits and demand subsides.

Should the US resurrect gold as the cornerstone of the international reserve system, decisions would have to be taken on the question of an official buying and selling price for gold. Under present conditions it would be extremely difficult to make the transition back to a fixed gold price system unless the official price was fixed initially well above the open-market price. If this were to happen, newly mined gold and gold from private holdings would tend to move to the US, matched by an outflow of dollars. This course would only be feasible if the US were running a balance of payments surplus, otherwise the consequences would be highly inflationary. There was, in fact, a parallel example in 1934 with the raising of the gold price by the US to the high figure of $35 per ounce.

To ensure longer-term stability it would be necessary for other countries to adopt official gold price mechanisms which would link their currencies to the US dollar by means of fixed parities. This, too, seems a difficult change to encompass at the present time in a world where exchange rates fluctuate by such wide margins. It is possible, however, there could be piecemeal adherence to the gold price and fixed exchange parity system as individual countries reached a point where adjustment could be made without adverse consequences for their currency exchange rates and internal economic prospects.

What seems certain is that the general adoption of a gold-based system with fixed parities will not be achieved by international negotiations under the aegis of the IMF. Because of the problems of reaching agreement, the more probable course would be for the US to take a unilateral decision to fix on gold or for a small number of countries to reach agreement to take a similar step.

Should there be a return to an official gold settlement system, one of the remaining problems would be the question of exchange rate fluctuation and adjustments. Again, it is highly improbable that there would be any return to the original Bretton Woods system with parities being maintained within a 2% band, and with restrictions over changes in official parities laid down by IMF regulations. With high rates of inflation and large differentials between the rates of cost and price inflation in different countries, the degree of day to day fluctuation in parities would need to be less restricted and, equally, central banks would need to establish a mechanism for adjusting official parities more frequently to reflect the divergencies in inflation between countries.

The more likely course is for solutions to evolve from current practice under the pressures of market forces. Centred around the EMU, the deutschemark bloc of currencies is now structured in such a way as to restrict the degree of day to day exchange rate fluctuations, at the same time providing opportunities for adjustment of official parities at frequent intervals. This system may hold the key to more widespread reform of the world's markets. The dollar bloc and deutschemark bloc could be brought more closely together towards a common system of official intervention to manage exchange rates within the more narrow limits operated under the EMU.

There is no reason why such a system could not be joined with the re-adoption of gold as an official reserve asset settlement between countries and international institutions. The attempt led by America in the early 1970s to demonetize gold has failed. The abandonment of the official gold price and the withdrawal of central banks from the gold market did not detract from the creditability of gold; on the contrary, the private demand for gold increased. Neither did governments dispose of gold from their official holdings to any significant extent and gold remains an extremely attractive collateral for central banks. At the enhanced price those reserves have an even greater importance.

This is not to deny the logic of arguments for demonetizing gold. Apart from its industrial use, gold as an investment is theoretically unattractive. It commands no rate of interest and entails safe custody charges. Over long periods the return on investment on gold has been negative in real terms and by a wide margin. It is only with the explosion of the gold price in the 1970s that investors have seen an attractive real return on their gold investments. Moreover, the supply of gold and newly mined gold can only contribute to the world's stocks at a slow pace. To base a world monetary system on an object where supply is erratic and not directly linked to the needs of the real world economy, is intellectually indefensible. The metal is not suitable as a common coinage and for the most part if remains locked up in bank vaults.

In theory, money should be a servant and not a master. In practice, the evidence of the centuries shows the reverse to be the case and down to the present day it remains true to say that money is master, though remaining an ingenious servant to the needs of commerce and exchange. It is equally illogical that gold, scattered capriciously around the world's surface, in finite supply and incapable of expansion at a pace commensurate with the growth in world output and trade in goods and services, should remain the universally accepted yardstick of value. But as we have seen the powerful logic of the argument for demonetization has been disregarded and rejected by the world's population. Gold has an enduring attraction and it is this which also makes it attractive for gold to feature as part of the world's official monetary system.

Should there be a return to an official price for gold, the problem which would need to be considered would be the level of gold holdings in relation to the growth of the world's economy. It is improbable, for example, that the potential increase in the world's gold supply could match the long-term rate of growth in the world's economy in real terms. Output growth for the world as a whole is unlikely to return to the fast rates of the post-war period up to 1973. The present slow rate of growth is unlikely to persist throughout the 1980s and we would anticipate a long-term average rate of growth in output for the world economy of between 3–4% per annum. The value of gold holdings ought to have some relationship to the growth in world output if price inflation is to be controlled effectively; thus, it might be necessary for the price of gold to rise by something like 2–3% per annum. This could be achieved in an orderly way in a return to a gold standard and one possibility is the adoption of a system for raising the official price of gold by a set amount each year—say, by 2%. This would ensure that the value of gold holdings in official exchange reserves would be less likely to diminish as a proportion of total reserves and the dangers of the emergence of a price differential in the free gold market would be reduced. This argument, however, would only be valid on the assumption that governments pursued rigorous policies of credit control which limited the rate of money expansion to the rate of growth of output in the real economies.

A return to gold, however, is not the only means of supplementing monetary assets in a world reserve system. Having in mind the limited supply of gold, a system based on other commodities with a durable character, such as silver, platinum or other high value metals, could be established. The only advantage of tangible assets of this kind as reserves would be to secure a more even supply of reserve assets from year to year. Even so, this solution probably has little to commend it since all metals enter into industrial production and commerce. Moreover, their scarcity value creates markets for collectors' items and so impinges on the availability of the materials for use as reserve assets.

We therefore suggest that such a diversification into commodity assets as reserves will be extremely unlikely. Our conclusion is, therefore, that gold will keep its importance in the world economy and will be retained as the key reserve asset in official holdings. We also argue that there is a strong chance of a return to a currency link with gold at some time in the 1980s.

The future of the dollar

We have argued that the US will remain the dominant world economic power through the remainder of the twentieth century and well into the next. We have also argued that the dominant position of the dollar as the world's most common unit of account and its preponderant position as a currency reserve asset will continue at least as long as the country's economic dominance. The proviso is that price inflation is successfully reduced and that there is no collapse of confidence in the currency.

There must still be a chance, in view of the complex network of pressures which make for rising inflation, that the current programme to curb inflation and return to something approaching currency stability could founder. The possible causes of such a failure would be a drastic increase in social unrest and violence linked with a dramatic rise in unemployment levels as a result of a deep recession.

The evidence of the nineteenth and twentieth centuries up to the Second World War is that inflation can be halted and indeed reversed at the cost of recession. The notable examples are the periods after the Napoleonic Wars and after the First World War. In the first case the example is probably worthless because of the utterly different nature of the economy at that time, and also because of the unreliability of the available statistics. Nevertheless, there can be no doubting the severity of the deflation and recession which succeeded in reversing and halting the inflation. The modern evidence suggests that a recession reducing output as a whole by as much as 5% might be necessary in order to break inflationary expectations and the inflation cycle. In Switzerland, for example, GNP fell by close to 7% in real terms in the mid-1970s when growth in the money supply was halted in an attempt to squeeze out inflation. Following a boom and a 10% average price rise in 1974, three years of severe monetary restraint brought the rate of retail price inflation down to a little more than 1%. Although on a limited scale, this example shows what may be required in other countries to achieve a reversal of the inflationary pressures. In Switzerland's case the brunt of the pressures of unemployment fell on the migrant workers rather than on the domestic population.

The example, however, may not particularly be relevant for the rest of the world. What we do not know is whether a high rate of unemployment—probably well over 10%—would be tolerated long enough to ensure the reduction of price inflation down to an average of 2 or 3% per annum, and whether the pressures to re-expand economies to create new jobs would lead to a resurgence of inflation. There is also the risk that an outbreak of war would trigger a surge in world commodity prices, driving up costs even faster, and that the accelerated military spending round the world and the bloated defence budgets would lead to huge increases in government deficit spending. As is usual in wartime, a large money inflation would be set in train to finance those deficits. In such an eventuality, of course, many countries would find themselves in the same difficulties, and it could well be that the relative position of the dollar would be unchanged.

Weighing all the factors, we come to the conclusion that there is an odds-on chance that inflation will be brought under control in the US and that the strict control of credit now being applied by the Federal Reserve will become a continuing policy. We argue that price inflation will decline erratically in the US from cycle to cycle throughout the 1980s and that progress in this direction will be sufficient to maintain international confidence in the dollar.

We also argue that, unless the US is involved in war, her balance of payments will improve and that the era of permanent US balance of payments deficit has come to an end. We believe the US economy is capable of transformation so as to achieve energy independence in the 1990s. In this regard the US will be better placed than the majority of world industrial powers, and this feature will contribute both to the improvement in the US balance of payments and the strengthening of confidence in the dollar.

This argument, therefore, must lead to the conclusion that the US dollar will remain the principal currency reserve asset in the world at large. This is not to say that there will not be changes in the world monetary order. We suggest that changes will evolve under the pressure of market forces, and we have little confidence that a new regime similar to the Bretton Woods system will be pieced together as a result of general international agreement. The IMF seems to be the wrong vehicle for achieving such an agreement.

World reform

The collapse of the Bretton Woods system led the world piecemeal into a regime of floating exchange rates in the 1970s. There were some similarities in this to the swing to floating arrangements in the 1930s. But in the 1970s the discipline of free floating rates had never been accepted because the swings in the price of currencies and the consequences for internal economies and international trade had seemed so great as to be unacceptable. What we have seen, therefore, is persistent official intervention in foreign exchange markets to smooth out the oscillations of floating rates.

Experience of floating exchange rates in the 1970s has not been particularly favourable and the oscillations in these rates have proved extremely unpopular in business circles. Sentiment, therefore, seems likely to swing in favour of a return to more active controls. The periodic fluctuation in systems and controls was commented on in a lecture by Mr C.W. McMahon, an Executive Director of the Bank of England, in 1978 as follows[2]:

> If we look back over the international monetary history of this century, I think we can detect an oscillation between more regulated and less regulated periods. Anyone who believes that history tends to repeat itself can predict with a good deal of conviction that we shall revert to a more regulated set of arrangements. But that facile prophecy evades the crucial question: what will be the appropriate set of rules for the post-floating period?

One interesting aspect of the pattern of change in the world's reserve and exchange system over time is whether or not we learn from history and previous mistakes. The individuals concerned with making decisions are obviously influenced by the experiences of their own careers within the short span of a working lifetime in responsible positions. It is to be doubted whether the experience of previous generations exerts much influence on current decisions. In the case of academic analysis, historical experience may be given greater weight, but then it is to be doubted whether such analysis really can contribute a great deal to the solution of current problems, since the personal experience of systems in the past is unlikely to be understood fully by those individuals responsible for taking decisions today.

What we have seen in this analysis is that systems evolve from year to year and from period to period very much under the influence of market pressures and forces. Market forces are ultimately paramount; confidence, or lack of it, tends to be based on fundamental values. Therefore, fundamental values such as cost and price differentials between countries and the resultant balance of payments developments, tend to be reflected in the market forces which ultimately shape the system. In this respect the development and growth of the Eurocurrency markets show the process of evolution at work and demonstrate how fundamental factors and market forces led us to a world system that replaced the crumbling edifice of the Bretton Woods structure. What now seems probable is that world exchange systems will evolve away from the present regime back towards a more closely regulated system with gold and the dollar as its cornerstones and with individual currencies fluctuating within controlled bands linked with some mechanism for frequent adjustment of official parities. In this respect changes in the world system will probably be achieved more easily and more swiftly if the US can return to the position of

[2]McMAHON, C.W. (June 1978). Is there an international monetary system? *Bank of England Quarterly Bulletin*. London.

dominance she enjoyed in the immediate post-war period and in the 1950s. To quote McMahon again:

> I believe, however, that the success of the Bretton Woods regime was due primarily to a fact more interesting, perhaps more fundamental, than these. At the heart of its early success lay the feature most severely criticized in its later stages: the asymmetry of the system and the unique role played in it by the US. At the end of the war, and for many years thereafter, no other major country remotely approached the size and power of the US; and she exercised this power in a strikingly beneficent and far-sighted way, which actively fostered the development of the rest of the industrialized world.

To get back to the position where the US dollar can be regarded as the bedrock on which the world's reserve system operates, there has to be not only the restoration of full confidence in the US, its economy and monetary management, but an adjustment in the world's market behaviour. McMahon put the problem as follows:

> Finally, there are the arguments of those who say the prime need is to stabilize the world's currencies. The case here centres primarily on the dollar, and the argument runs that our difficulties stem from the fact that ...the US has taken a place as a regular participant in the adjustment game while continuing her role as the banker. Movements in the dollar exchange rate that might be justified on balance of payments grounds become more dangerous, it is argued, in the effects they have on the value of what is effectively the world's only reserve asset. In a sense, those who argue in this way are asking whether in the long run, in the light of developing changes in relative power, the US will be willing to continue alone to shoulder the burden of providing the world's reserve assets.

We would argue that with the restoration of the role of gold at its enhanced price, the reserve role of the dollar would be unlikely to prove a burden to the US. This assumes, of course, that she is willing in any case to follow policies aimed at keeping the rate of price inflation to an acceptably low level.

We would therefore summarize the prospect for the dollar and the world reserve system as follows:

(1) The US will remain the leading world economy throughout the rest of the century and will not be overtaken by the EEC or Japan.
(2) The enshrinement of national sovereignty within the Treaty of Rome will ensure that progress towards full economic union by the Common Market will be painfully slow, and that a common currency operated by an EEC central bank is unlikely to be achieved until the 1990s, if at all.
(3) The EEC will be outpaced in economic expansion by the US and Canada in terms of world trade and commerce, and the majority of transactions will continue to be designated in US dollars.
(4) Eurocurrency markets will continue to supply the needs for developing countries and the recycling of payments surpluses around the world, leaving the IMF with the lesser role of lender of last resort to countries with payments difficulties.
(5) The SDR will not be expanded to become the world's major reserve asset, although the simplification of the SDR basket of currencies will reduce

the inconvenience of the SDR as an exchange unit. Even so, a 'substitution account' for exchanging surplus dollars into SDRs is unlikely to be established. The SDR may well be retained as a convenient *numéraire* or unit of account between countries, but this will depend on whether gold is restored at an official fixed price as an international reserve asset. If this were to happen, reserves could once again be expressed in terms of the US dollar, unless the price of gold itself were officially fixed in terms of the SDR.

(6) The EMU is unlikely to become a world reserve asset although the European Monetary System, ensuring more narrow swings in exchange rates between the participating member countries, may be more widely adopted as a system for regulating exchange parities and movements between the world's leading currencies.

(7) Further diversification of currency reserves into the deutschemark, Swiss franc, terling, yen and the French franc is highly likely, though not on such a scale as to reduce the central role of the US dollar.

(8) There is a possibility, which would tend to strengthen the position of the dollar, of the US unilaterally adopting an officially fixed gold price and that such a move would be followed by other countries, thus facilitating a return to a more orderly regime of fixed parities. Progress along this direction will depend upon the rate of success in curbing inflation and in narrowing inflation differentials between countries. It is also likely that on a return to something approaching a fixed parity system, more frequent adjustment in parities will be adopted than were permitted under the original Bretton Woods agreement, and that the degree of fluctuation around the central parity would be wider.

Finally, due account must be taken of the network of committees at work involving central banks, the IMF and BIS which constitute an effective forum for discussing possibilities of change and the adoption of new systems. Although agreement between large numbers of countries will remain extremely difficult to achieve, informal discussion could lead to the conviction in official circles in the US of the need to change and to adopt a new system. If that conviction is sufficiently strong, then unilateral action by the US could result in the general introduction of a reform of the world system, reflecting the ideas being discussed in the various international committees. In all of this it is to be hoped that the lessons learned from the inflationary past, particularly with regard to the undisciplined expansion of bank credit, will be heeded and that governments and their central banks will institute far more rigorous controls over domestic banks and the creation of credit in the future. Such changes in practice will be essential for the curbing and reduction of inflation and, without them, changes towards an ordered world monetary and exchange system will be painfully slow and dangerous.

It is to be hoped that valuable lessons have now been learned, at least to some extent, giving grounds for cautious optimism that a more ordered system could well emerge during the 1980s, leading to far more stable conditions in the 1990s and beyond. Thus, throughout the next generation there must be a high probability of the world remaining on a US dollar standard and with a renewed link to gold.

Postscript

The composition of the SDR was revised during 1980 and from 1 January 1981 has been as follows:

Composition of the SDR from 1 January 1981

	(%)
US dollar	42
Deutschemark	19
Sterling	13
French franc	13
Japanese yen	13
	100

The revised basket is close to that previously used to determine the rate of interest on the SDR. The change has been made well ahead of the review planned for 1983 in order to unify and simplify the system.

The revision was prompted for the additional reason that a simplified SDR would encourage a trend towards its use as a unit of account in private capital markets. Since the five component currencies are widely traded currencies this appears to be feasible and the use of the SDR can be expected to expand.

That being the case, the IMF would itself be able to borrow directly from the private capital markets via the issue of bonds denominated in SDRs. It is no coincidence that in addition to the US dollar, the deutschemark and sterling have begun to feature as an international reserve asset in spite of the unwillingness of the German and British authorities to see their currencies used in this capacity. The change in the composition of the SDR therefore reflects the *de facto* change in international asset management towards multiple foreign exchange reserve assets.

It is now planned to review the composition of the SDR basket at five-year intervals from 1 January 1986.

A disadvantage of the revision is that the revised SDR unit will not provide such a wide hedge against currency fluctuation. But this would appear to be a minor factor. Of more significance, the spread in the commercial use of the

SDR is likely to strengthen the lending powers of the IMF by giving it access to a more diversified range of widely traded currencies. This, in turn, will lessen the dependence on the US dollar as a reserve asset.

The change in commercial practice during 1980 was of some significance, more than a dozen London banks accepting SDR-denominated deposits. Some banks began to provide forward exchange cover for SDRs and a small SDR inter-bank market was established, which will probably expand to substantial proportions.

To set the SDR in perspective, as was discussed in Chapter 9, world reserves are dominated by gold and the dollar, the SDR accounting for little more than 2½% of total world reserves in 1980.

Bibliography

ALEXANDER, S.S. (1952). Effects of Devaluation on a Trade Balance. *IMF Staff Papers*. Washington, DC

BAGEHOT, W. (1931). *Lombard Street*. London; John Murray

BANK OF ENGLAND. *Quarterly Bulletins*. London

BIS. Bank for International Settlements. *Annual Reports*. Basle

BAREAU, P. (1958). The Future of the Sterling System. *Institute of Economic Affairs Readings*. London

BAREAU, P. (1979). The International Money and Capital Markets. *Institute of Economic Affairs Readings 19*. London

BELL, G.L. (1973). *The Euro-Dollar Market and the International Financial System*. New York; Macmillan

BERMAN, P.I. (1978). *Inflation and the Money Supply in the United States 1956–1977*. Mass.; Lexington Books

BLADEN, A. (1980). *How to cope with the Developing Financial Crisis*. New York; McGraw Hill

BLAINEY, G. (1958). *Gold and Paper*. Melbourne; National Bank of Australasia

BLOOMFIELD, A.I. (1959). *Monetary Policy Under the International Gold Standard, 1800–1914*. New York; Federal Reserve Bank

THE BRANDT COMMISSION (1980). *North—South*. London; Pan Books

BRITISH PETROLEUM (BP). *Statistical Review of the Oil Industry*. London. Annual editions

CARR-SAUNDERS, A.M. (1936). *World Population: Past Growth and Present Trends*. Oxford University Press

CLARKE, W.M. (1965). The City in the World Economy. *Institute of Economic Affairs Readings*. London

COBBETT, W. (1830). *Rural Rides in the Counties of Surrey, Kent, Sussex, etc.* London (Republished by Penguin; Harmondsworth)

COLE, G.D.H. (1944). *Money: Its Present and Future*. London; Cassell

CROCKETT, A.D. and GOLDSTEIN, M. (1976). Inflation under fixed and flexible exchange rates. *IMF Staff Papers*. Washington, DC

CROCKETT, A.D. (1977). *International Money*. London; Nelson

CUNLIFFE COMMITTEE (1919). *Fiscal Report*. Command Paper 464; London; HMSO

DEANE, P. and COLE, W.A. (1969). *British Economic Growth, 1868–1959.* Cambridge University Press

DOWNES, A. (1979). Population Explosion — of Automobiles. *Across the Board.* New York; The Conference Board

DUNN, R.M. Jr (1973). Exchange Rate Rigidity, Investment Distortions and the Future of Bretton Woods. *Princeton Essays in International Finance No. 97*

EINZIG, P. (1970). *The Eurodollar System.* London; Macmillan

EINZIG, P. (1970). *The History of Foreign Exchange.* London; Macmillan

EMDEN, P.H. (1937). *Money Powers in Europe in the Nineteenth and Twentieth Centuries.* London; Sampson Low

EMMINGER, O. (1967). Practical aspects of the problem of balance of payments adjustment. *Journal of Political Economy*

ENOCH, C.A. (1979). The direction of causality between the exchange rate, prices and money. *Bank of England Discussion Paper No. 7.* London

FEAVEARYEAR, A.E. (1931). *The Pound Sterling.* Oxford University Press

FLEMING, J.M. (1975). Reflections on the International Monetary Reform. *Princeton Essays in International Finance No. 107*

FRENKEL, J.A. and JOHNSON, H.G. (1976). *The Monetary Approach to the Balance of Payments.* London; Allen and Unwin

FRIEDMAN, M. (1953). The Case for Flexible Exchange Rates. *Essays in Positive Economics.* University of Chicago Press

FRIEDMAN, M. (1969). *The Eurodollar Market: Some First Principles.* New York; Morgan Guarantee Survey

FRIEDMAN, M. and ROOSA, R.V. (1967). *The Balance of Payments: Free vs Fixed Exchange Rates.* American Enterprise Institute. Washington, DC

FRIEDMAN, M. and SCHWARZ, A. (1963). *A Monetary History of the United States, 1867–1960.* Princeton University Press

GILBERT, M. (1968). The Gold Dollar System: Conditions of Equilibrium and the Price of Gold. *Princeton Essays in International Finance No. 70*

GLYNN, C. (1979). Gold 1979. *Consolidated Goldfields Annual Gold Market Studies.* London

GRUBEL, H. (1971). The demand for international reserves: a critical review of the literature. *Journal of Economic Literature.*

HALM, G.N. (1975). *A Guide to International Monetary Reform.* Mass.; Lexington Books

HARROD, R.F. (1969). *Money.* London; Macmillan

HELLEINER, G. (1975). The less-developed countries and the international monetary system. *Journal of Development Studies*

HEWSON, J.R. and SAKAKIBARA, E. (1975). *Eurocurrency Markets and their Implications.* Mass.; Lexington Books

HEWSON, J.R. (1975). *Liquidity Creation and Distribution in the Eurocurrency Markets.* Mass.; Lexington Books

HIRSCH, F. (1969). *Money International.* Harmondsworth; Penguin

HODGMAN, D.R. (1974). *National Monetary Policies and International Monetary Co-operation.* Boston; Little Brown

INTERNATIONAL MONETARY FUND (1970). *International Reserves: Needs and Availability.* Washington, DC; IMF

INTERNATIONAL MONETARY FUND (1970). *The Reform of the International Monetary System.* Report by the Executive Directors. Washington, DC; IMF

INTERNATIONAL MONETARY FUND (1974). *International Monetary Reform: Documents of the Committee of Twenty*. Washington, DC; IMF

ISHIYAMA, Y. (1975). *Optimum Currency Areas: A Survey*. Washington, DC. IMF Staff Papers

KATZ, S.I. (1972). The Case for the Par Value System, 1972. *Princeton Essays in International Finance No. 92*

KEYNES, J.M. (1923). *A Tract on Monetary Reform*. London; Macmillan

KEYNES, J.M. (1934). *A Treatise on Money*. London; Macmillan

KINDLEBERGER, C.P. (1966). *Europe and the Dollar*. Cambridge, Mass.; MIT Press

LAFFER, A.B. and MEISELMAN, D. (Eds.) (1975). *The Phenomenon of Worldwide Inflation*. Washington, DC; American Enterprise Institute

LANYI, A. (1969). The Case for the Floating Exchange Rates Reconsidered. *Princeton Essays in International Finance No. 72*

LEVY, M.E. (1980). Guns and a Little Margarine Too. *Across the Board*. New York; The Conference Board

MACHLUP, F. (1970). Euro-dollar creation: a mystery story. *Banca Nazionale del Laboro Quarterly Review*

MACHLUP, F. (1964). Plans for the Reform of the International Monetary System. *Princeton Special Papers in International Economics No. 3*

McMAHON, C.W. (1976). Controlling the Euromarkets. *Bank of England Quarterly Bulletin*. London

MEADE, J.E. (1951). *The Balance of Payments*. Oxford University Press

MEADE, J.E. (1955). The Case for Variable Exchange Rates. *Three Banks Review*. London

MENDELSOHN, M.S. (1980). *Money on the Move*. New York; McGraw Hill

MORRELL, J.G. (1980). *Britain through the 1980s*. Farnborough, Hants.; Gower Publishing

MORSE, C.J. (1974). The Evolving Monetary System. *IMF Survey*. Washington, DC

NEWTON, ISAAC (1717). *Report* by Sir Isaac Newton as Master of the Mint, dated 21 September 1717. Republished in *Select Tracts and Documents illustrative of English Monetary History*. London; W.A. Shaw (1896)

NIEHAUS, J. and HEWSON, J. (1976). The Euro-dollar Market and Monetary Theory. *Journal of Money, Credit and Banking*

PEARCE, A.W. (1979). World Energy Prospects. *Esso Magazine No. 110*. London

PHELPS BROWN, E.H. and HOPKINS, S. (1956). Seven Centuries of the Price of Consumables compared with Builders' Wage Rates. *Economica*. London

ROOSA, R.V. (1967). *The Dollar and World Liquidity*. New York; Random House

ROSTOW, W.W. (1978). *The World Economy, History and Prospects*. New York; McMillan

RUEFF, J. and HIRSCH, F. (1965). The Rule and the Role of Gold: An Argument. *Princeton Essays in International Finance No. 47*

SAVILLE, I.D. (1980). The Sterling/Dollar Rate in the Floating Rate Period: the Role of Money, Prices and Intervention. *Bank of England Discussion Paper No. 9*. London

SOHMEN, E. (1961). *Flexible Exchange Rates: Theory and Controversy*. University of Chicago Press

TRIFFIN, R. (1960). *Gold and the Dollar Crisis.* New Haven, Conn.; Yale University Press

TRIFFIN, R. (1967). *Our International Monetary System — Yesterday, Today and Tomorrow.* New York; Random House

WALLICH, H.C. (1979). The Inflation Syndrome. *Across the Board.* New York; The Conference Board

WHITMAN, M. (1975). Global Monetarism and the Monetary Approach to the Balance of Payments. *Brooking Papers in Economic Activity No. 3.* Brookings Institution, Washington, DC

WILLIAMS, J. (1965). The Crawling Peg. *Princeton Essays in International Finance No. 50*

WITTEVEEN, H.J. (1975). *Inflation and the International Monetary System. American Economic Review*

Index